HAPPY HUNTING

HAPPY HUNTING

A New
Musical Comedy

Book by
Howard Lindsay
and
Russel Crouse

Lyrics by
Matt Dubey
Music by
Harold Karr

Random House
New York

To Ethel Merman,
to whom we, too, are dedicated

HAPPY HUNTING *was first presented by Jo Mielziner at the Majestic Theatre on the evening of December 6, 1956, with the following cast:*

(In order of appearance)

SANFORD STEWART, JR.	Gordon Polk
MRS. SANFORD STEWART, SR.	Olive Templeton
JOSEPH	Mitchell M. Gregg
BETH LIVINGSTONE	Virginia Gibson
JACK ADAMS, a reporter	Seth Riggs
HARRY WATSON, a reporter	Gene Wesson
CHARLIE, a photographer	Delbert Anderson
LIZ LIVINGSTONE	Ethel Merman
SAM	Clifford Fearl
JOE	John Craig
FREDDY	George Martin
WES	Jim Hutchison
MARY MILLS	Estelle Parsons
DICK DAVIS	Robert C. Held
BOB GRAYSON	Carl Nicholas
MAUD FOLEY	Mary Finney
POLICE SERGEANT	Mark Zeller
ARTURO	Leon Belasco
THE DUKE OF GRANADA	Fernando Lamas
COUNT CARLOS	Renato Cibelli
WAITER	Don Weissmuller
SHIP'S OFFICER	John Leslie
BARMAN	Warren J. Brown
MRS. B	Florence Dunlap
MRS. D.	Madeleine Clive
MRS. L.	Kelley Stephens
TERENCE, a groom	Jim Hutchison

SAM, JOE, FREDDY, WES — photographers

MARY MILLS, DICK DAVIS, BOB GRAYSON — reporters

TOM, a groom	Eugene Louis
DAISY	Moe
MR. T., a member of the Hunt	John Leslie
MR. M., a member of the Hunt	Jay Velie
ALBERT, a groom	George Martin
MARGARET, a maid	Mara Landi

Directed by Abe Burrows
Settings by Jo Mielziner
Costumes by Irene Sharaff
Choreography by Alex Romero and Bob Herget
Musical direction by Jay Blackton
Stage managed by Robert Downing

SCENES

MUSICAL PROGRAM

ACT ONE

Overture	
Postage-Stamp Principality	Tourists and Monegasques
Don't Tell Me	Sandy and Beth
Gee, but It's Good to Be Here	Liz and the Reporters
Mutual Admiration Society	Liz and Beth
For Love or Money	The Girls
Bikini Dance	Beth
It's Like a Beautiful Woman	The Duke
Wedding-of-the-Year Blues	Maud, Harry, Jack, the reporters and photographers
Mr. Livingstone	Liz
If'n	Beth, Sandy and the Passengers
This Is What I Call Love	Liz

ACT TWO

A New-Fangled Tango	Liz, Beth, Arturo and the Guests
She's Just Another Girl	Sandy
The Game of Love	Liz
Happy Hunting	Liz, the Duke and members of the Hunt
I'm a Funny Dame	Liz
This Much I Know	The Duke
Just Another Guy	Liz
Everyone Who's "Who's Who"	Jack, Harry and the Footmen
Mutual Admiration Society—Reprise	Liz and the Duke

HAPPY HUNTING

ACT ONE

ACT ONE

SCENE 1

Outside the palace gates in Monaco.
We are attracted first to a group of schoolgirls who enter
gingerly and peer up at the palace in adolescent awe. The
Wedding, which put Monaco's romantic postage stamps in every
collector's album, is imminent and the girls sing, with youthful
pride, "Postage-Stamp Principality."

(GIRLS)
O, this fairy tale romance
O, the pomp and circumstance
On this day of days in this happy little land
A fairy tale princess weds a prince
At the wedding of the century
In this pint-sized, pin-point, pre-shrunk, postage-stamp
Principality

The bride-to-be will be
Two times a princess
Four times a duchess
Nine times a baroness
Eight times a countess
Four times a marchioness
And a hundred and eleven times a lady

3

O, let joy overwhelm
This three-hundred-seventy-acre realm
Point five nine square miles, half the size of Central Park
A fairy tale in a fairyland
A modern Cinderella story

> (*At this point in the song the lights come up and the stage comes alive with the people who have been attracted to Monaco by The Wedding—tourists, reporters, photographers, and international types and celebrities of varied importance, typified, for example, by one who closely resembles Farouk, the former King of Egypt. These all join in the song.*)

In this pint-sized, pin-point, pre-shrunk, postage-stamp
Principality

With the population's cheers
And the singing ringing in their ears
They will wave farewell from their virginal white
One-hundred-and-thirty-eight-foot yacht
And sail off into the sunlit sea
From this fairy tale kingdom
Diminutive dominion
Rococo little country
Miniature monarchy
This itsy-bitsy
Teensy-weensy
Pint-sized, pin-point, pre-shrunk, postage-stamp
Principality.

> (*At the end of the number, the group disperses, some leaving the scene, others forming in small groups.* MRS.

SANFORD STEWART, SR., *enters. She is a* grande dame *of the Philadelphia Main Line. With her is her son,* SANFORD STEWART, JR., *known as* SANDY, *an attractive, young Philadelphia lawyer. As they cross, they meet, midstage, a man who recognizes them. His name is* JOSEPH.)

JOSEPH

Hello, Mr. Stewart!
(SANDY *looks at him, obviously bewildered, then does the courteous thing, by greeting him with the overenthusiasm you reserve for people you can't quite place.*)

SANDY

Hello, there! How are you? I didn't know you were over here.

JOSEPH

I knew you were abroad.
(JOSEPH *bows to* MRS. STEWART.)

SANDY

Mother—this is—(*He's stuck for the name, so turns to* JO-SEPH) You remember my mother!

MRS. STEWART

(*Pleasantly, but distinctly not cordial*)
How do you do?

JOSEPH

Are you here for the wedding, Mrs. Stewart?

MRS. STEWART

Oh, dear, no! We're not here for the wedding.

5

SANDY

How did you leave things—in Philadelphia?

JOSEPH

Fine.

MRS. STEWART

(*Dismissingly*)

It was nice to have seen you.

SANDY

Yes. Yes.

JOSEPH

Thank you. *Au revoir.*
      (*He bows and exits.*)

SANDY

Au revoir. I know I know him.

MRS. STEWART

Of course you know him. He's a headwaiter at the Philadelphia Club.

SANDY

Well, we may get better service.

MRS. STEWART

Sandy, I'm going back to the hotel. There are so many dubious Philadelphians here. I should never have come.

6

SANDY

I'll walk back with you.

MRS. STEWART

No, Sandy, you might see another familiar face and I don't want to be introduced to an upstairs maid.
(She starts offstage right, and SANDY *starts with her.* BETH LIVINGSTONE, *an attractive girl about twenty, enters right. She sees* SANDY *and recognizes him.)*

BETH
(As she passes him)

Hello, Mr. Stewart.

MRS. STEWART

Good-bye, Sandy.
(She exits. SANDY *turns to* BETH, *uncertain again and more cautious.)*

SANDY

Hello, there!

BETH

You don't remember me, do you?

SANDY

Don't remember you? Why certainly. You're—you're—
(He hestitates.)

BETH

Would it help if I told you who you are? You're Sanford Stewart—Philadelphia Assembly, City Troop, Radnor Hunt

7

Club, Yale, Harvard Law School, now with Lippincott, Lippincott, Drexel and Lippincott. Right?

SANDY

Right! And you're . . .
> (BETH *starts to answer but he puts his hand up to stop her, and sings, "Don't Tell Me.")*

> (SANDY)

Uh-h-h-h-h-h-h-h
Don't tell me
I know, I know
I know
It's right on the tip of my—Isabel!
No, no. Don't I know you from somewhere?
I know I know you from somewhere, but where?
Eh-h-h-h-h-h-h-h
Don't tell me
I know, I know
I know
Just give me a minute, I'll—Harriet!
No, no. Didn't you used to be skinny? Wear braces?
I'm very bad at remembering names
But I never forget—
No, don't tell me
I know, I know
I know
I remember I danced with you to a mambo band
That's it! That's it!

> (BETH)

That's not it.

8

HAPPY HUNTING

(SANDY)
And
That's not it!
Was it Paris or Rome?

(BETH)
I met you . . .

(SANDY)
London or home?

(BETH)
I let you . . .

(SANDY)
No, don't tell me
I know, I know
I know
Sure, I drove you home from a barbecue
And I told you I had a flat
And you thought that I was a rat
Don't tell me
I know, I know
I know
As improbable as it seems
I know I've met you in my dreams

(BETH)
Don't tell me
I know, I know

(SANDY)

I know . . .
This is a breeze!
No, don't tell me
No, don't tell me?
No! Don't! Tell me, please!

(*At the end of the song, two reporters,* JACK ADAMS *and* HARRY WATSON, *enter. With them is* CHARLIE, *a photographer.* JACK *stops as he reaches* BETH *and* SANDY.)

JACK

Hello, Mr. Stewart. (*To* BETH) Hello, there.

BETH

Hello.

(SANDY *is still trying to remember who* BETH *is.*)

JACK

(*To* BETH)

I'm Jack Adams of the Philadelphia *Inquirer*. You're here for the wedding?

BETH

I wouldn't miss it. Mother and I got in last night.

JACK

Your mother here? (*To* HARRY) Her mother's always good for a story.

HARRY

I'll be the judge of that. Who is her mother?

JACK

(*To* BETH)

Don't be offended. He's with the Chicago *Tribune*. (*To* HARRY) Her mother is the most fabulous woman in Philadelphia.

SANDY

(*Suddenly acting as though a bolt of lightning had struck him*)

Beth Livingstone! That's who you are—Beth Livingstone! You're Beth Livingstone!

BETH

Don't tell me!

JACK

(*Introducing* SANDY *to* HARRY)

This is Sanford Stewart. Harry Watson.

SANDY

(*Putting his hand out genially*)

How do you do?

HARRY

(*Addressing* JACK *and ignoring* SANDY's *outstretched hand completely*)

Jack, who's the girl's mother?

JACK

She's Liz Livingstone. Haven't you heard about the Third World War?

(*During all this,* SANDY *keeps his hand outstretched and the smile fixed on his face. He is stuck with his greeting, but, being a gentleman, there is nothing he can do about it.*)

HARRY

Which one?

JACK

The war between Liz Livingstone and the Philadelphia Main Line.

HARRY

Just tell me one thing. Who is Liz Livingstone?

BETH

(*To* HARRY)
Only the best businessman in Philadelphia.

JACK

Five years ago she almost cornered the stock of the Pennsylvania Railroad.

HARRY

Hadn't she ever ridden on it?

JACK

What she wanted to do was make the Main Line a branch line.

HARRY

This dame sounds like good copy. Where is she?

BETH

The last time I saw Mother she was shooting dice with Mr. Onassis. She believes in going right to the top.

HARRY

Let's go!

JACK
(*To the photographer*)
Get some pictures, Charlie.
(*He indicates* BETH *and* SANDY, *and starts out.*)

HARRY
(*Following him*)
Nice to have met you, Mr. ——

SANDY

Stewart.
(JACK *and* HARRY *exit.* SANDY *waves good-bye.*)

CHARLIE
(*To* BETH *and* SANDY)
Okay. Over here.
(*They move where he has indicated.*)

BETH
(*To* SANDY)
You're not here for the wedding?

SANDY

No, I'm here on business. My firm, Lippincott, Lippincott . . .

BETH

Drexel and—

SANDY

—Lippincott, represents the syndicate that runs one of the hotels here, and I'm sort of checking up on . . .

CHARLIE

A little closer. Go into a clinch.

SANDY

A clinch?

BETH

Main Liners don't clinch.
(*There is a commotion offstage and* CHARLIE *looks off, then forgets* SANDY *and* BETH.)

CHARLIE

Grace Kelly!
(*Voices are heard offstage, calling, "Oh, Miss Kelly!" "Just a minute, Miss Kelly!" "Please, Your Grace, just one picture!" "Miss Kelly!"* CHARLIE *rushes over just as two or three photographers back onstage ahead of a small feminine figure wearing a dark blue coat with a large white hat, the rim of which covers her face. She is carrying a toy black poodle. More photographers and reporters follow her. She is trying to get through this crowd to the palace gates, and is blocked at every turn. She tries some broken-field running but is hemmed in and finally stopped by a couple of photographers lying flat on the ground trying to shoot up under the big hat. Finally she gives up, pushes back the hat and reveals that she is not Grace Kelly but* LIZ LIVINGSTONE.)

LIZ

All right! All right! So it ain't Kelly under the kelly.

SECOND PHOTOGRAPHER

It's Liz Livingstone!

MARY MILLS (A REPORTER)

Hey! What a woman!
(*The crowd starts drifting off.*)

BETH

Mother! What are you up to now?

LIZ

I was trying to get into the palace. I can't get anybody on the telephone. I asked for Margaret, I asked for Jack, I asked for Grace. And the dumb cluck on the other end kept saying, "His Grace is not to be disturbed." So I let him have it. (*To photographers and reporters*) And you can quote me! I said, "She isn't his Grace. She's still Philadelphia's Grace!"

BETH

Mother, when they say "His Grace," they mean the Prince.

LIZ

Is his name Grace, too? (*She gives her hat to* BETH) Here, take this skimmer back to the hotel.

BETH

(*Indicating* SANDY)
Mother, you remember Mr. Stewart.

15

LIZ

Oh, yes, you work for my lawyers. I can use you. Take care of this.

(*She hands him the toy dog.*)

CHARLIE

Mrs. Livingstone, may we have some pictures?

LIZ

Why not?

(*She removes her coat and gives it to* BETH. *The photographers start shooting.*)

BETH

(*To* SANDY)

Come on. I'll let you buy me a drink.

SANDY

Beth Livingstone!

(*They exit.*)

MARY MILLS

Mrs. Livingstone, what do you think of the wedding?

LIZ

I'll give you the same statement I gave Jinx Falkenburg. Today this is a land of . . .

CHARLIE

Would you stand over here, Mrs. Livingstone?

16

LIZ

(She crosses several steps right, and resumes)

Today this is a land of dreams come true. It's a storybook romance—this marriage between European nobility and a simple, wholesome American girl—even if she was in pictures. This may not have—(CHARLIE *grabs her chin and turns her head*) This may not have occurred to you, but to me she's Cinderella and he's Prince Charming. And you can quote me on that. Yes, all the world has taken these two lovers to its heart. Today—(*There is a chord from the orchestra*) this is the only place in all the world—(*Another chord*) to be.

(LIZ *bursts into song, "Gee, but It's Good to Be Here"*)

Gee, but it's good to be here
Frankly, I feel right at home
Here is where all the excitement is
This is champagne with all the fizz

Gee, but it's good to be here
I really feel in rare form
There's nothing like this, not anywhere
There's a magic that's in the air

I'm so ecstatic
I could yell, I could dance about
To be emphatic
I could shout, shout, shout, shout, shout, it out

Oh gee, but it's good to be here
Wouldn't miss this for the world
It's my considered opinion that

The place to be is the place I'm at
And I couldn't be more sincere
Gee, but it's good to be here!

Gee, but it's good to be here
Frankly, I feel right at home
And if you want to know what I think
What I think is I'm tickled pink

(REPORTERS *and* PHOTOGRAPHERS)
Gee, but it's good to be here
You really feel in rare form

(LIZ)
I'm like a kid in a candy store
This is what I've been waiting for
I'm so ecstatic
I could howl, I could yell it out

(REPORTERS *and* PHOTOGRAPHERS)
Let's be emphatic

(LIZ)
What's not to be happy about?

(REPORTERS *and* PHOTOGRAPHERS)
You could shout, shout, shout, shout, shout it out

(LIZ)
Oh gee, but it's good to be here!

(REPORTERS *and* PHOTOGRAPHERS)

Here is just where you belong

(LIZ)

It's my considered opinion that
The place to be is the place I'm at
And I couldn't be more sincere
Gee, but it's good to be
    Swell to be
    Great to be

(ALL)

Gee, but it's good to be here!

MARY

Thank you, Mrs. Livingstone—that's great. Boys, get some
more pictures.

(*The reporters exit.* MAUD FOLEY *enters from the
palace. She is also from Philadelphia, but not a Main
Liner.*)

MAUD

Newspaper photographers! Oh, I suppose you want to take
my picture again.

LIZ

Maud!

MAUD

Liz!

LIZ

Did you just come from the palace?

MAUD

This very minute. (*To the photographers*) Where do you want me to stand?

SECOND PHOTOGRAPHER

Somewhere away from Mrs. Livingstone. We're taking her picture.

MAUD

But, I'm Mrs. T. Joseph Foley. Don't you remember? (*Proudly*) I was robbed of a hundred thousand dollars' worth of jewels.

SECOND PHOTOGRAPHER

Lady, that was three days ago.

LIZ

Maud, forget it. Did you do what I asked you? Did you find out anything?

MAUD

Yes, but I'm afraid I'm in the way here.
(*She starts off but* LIZ *holds her.*)

LIZ

You can take us together. Mrs. Foley's my oldest friend.

MAUD

Make that best friend—not oldest.

LIZ

Maud—what friend have I got that's older than you?

CHARLIE

Look over here.

LIZ

What did you find out? I just left the hotel and our wedding invitations aren't there yet.

MAUD

Yes, I know.

LIZ

Have you seen Grace? Have you seen her mother? Have you told them we're here?
(*Throughout this scene* LIZ *and* MAUD *are changing poses for the photographers, with every sentence.*)

MAUD

Liz, it's the day before the wedding. You can't get near them.

SECOND PHOTOGRAPHER

Over the shoulders, please.
(LIZ *and* MAUD *turn and look over their shoulders.*)

LIZ

You mean you haven't any news for us?

CHARLIE

This way, please.
(*They turn back.*)

MAUD

Yes, I have. I got a list of the wedding guests and I checked it.

21

LIZ

Yes?

MAUD

Your names aren't on it!
(LIZ's *face falls*.)

LIZ

What do you mean, our names aren't on it?

MAUD

Liz, you and Beth are not invited to the wedding.

LIZ

Not invited. You can't mean that.

SECOND PHOTOGRAPHER

Can't you give us a smile, Mrs. Livingstone?
(LIZ *gives them a sickly smile*.)

CHARLIE

Now stand over here, please.

LIZ

Boys, no more pictures.

CHARLIE

Just one more.

LIZ

Enough's enough, and you've got enough.

SECOND PHOTOGRAPHER

Okay, Mrs. Livingstone, thanks.

THIRD PHOTOGRAPHER

I was out of film anyway.

(*The photographers exit.*)

LIZ

Maud, this is terrible! How am I going to tell Beth? It's going to break her heart. When her father died—Beth was only two years old—I promised him—"Mr. Livingstone," I said, "I'll see that Beth—"

MAUD

I know just how you feel, Liz.

LIZ

I can't face telling her. I've got to figure out something. Beth must never know we weren't invited. How could the Kellys do this to us?

MAUD

Well, Liz, they had to take care of the International Set.

LIZ

The International Set! You mean bums like that unfrocked Farouk? People like him sitting there, watching a nice American girl—one of our great movie stars—being married off to a foreigner. That's what the guy is—a foreigner. Every place in the world but here, he's a foreigner!

MAUD

He's a prince.

LIZ

A prince of what? This whole joint isn't as big as Franklin Field. Maud, I'll get even if it's the last thing I do.

MAUD

Liz, you can't top this wedding.

LIZ

I can't, can't I?
(JACK *and* HARRY *enter.*)

JACK

There she is—that's Liz Livingstone.

HARRY

(*To* LIZ)

Mrs. Livingstone, I'm Harry Watson of the Chicago *Tribune*.

MAUD

(*Starting out*)

See you later, Liz.

JACK

(*To* MAUD)

Just a minute! Aren't you Mrs. T. Joseph Foley?

MAUD

No! Revere's the name. Mrs. Paul Revere.
(*She exits.*)

HARRY

We've been looking for you, Mrs. Livingstone, and we'd like a quote from you on the wedding.

LIZ

You mean something that could be printed?

HARRY

Of course.

LIZ

Well, for publication, I'd say—
    (LIZ *sings*)
Gee, but it's good to be here
Wouldn't miss this for the world
Get this sunny smile on my face
I'm in love with the Prince and Grace
So three cheers for Princess Rainier
Gee, but it's good to be here!
    (*She exits.*)
           (*Blackout*)

Scene 2

Sitting room of LIZ LIVINGSTONE'S *suite at the Hotel Riviera. At rise,* BETH *is talking on the telephone, which is on a desk in the center of the room. There is a door, right, leading to the bedrooms and another, left, leading to the outer corridor.*

BETH

(*Into telephone*)

Well, I'm not sure how it happened—I was out riding—but they stole all our clothes—every stitch we own. (*There is a knock on the door*) Entrez! (*Into telephone*) The police are with Mother now.

(HARRY WATSON *and* MARY MILLS *enter.*)

MARY

(*Excited*)

Miss Livingstone, is it true your mother's been robbed?

(BETH *holds up her hand to indicate she is not to be interrupted.*)

BETH

(*Into telephone*)

Well, Mrs. Waldron, you're the same size as Mother—

HARRY

They told us down at the police station that your mother had been robbed!

BETH

(*To* HARRY)

Yes, she was. (*Into telephone*) If you could just lend Mother something to wear—

HARRY

(*Impatient*)

Come on, Miss Livingstone, we've got to file a story!

BETH

(*Into telephone*)

I don't know whether Mother would prefer the red one or the green one.

HARRY

Take the green one.

MARY

The red one.

BETH

(*Into telephone*)

We'll take the red one.
    (*She hangs up.*)

HARRY

(*Hot on the story*)

Now, what happened, Miss Livingstone?

MARY

Yes, how much did they get?

BETH

You'll have to talk to the police. I've got to borrow something for Mother to wear. All she has now is a pair of pajamas. (*She starts for the door.*)

HARRY

But, Miss Livingstone—

BETH

I'll be right back.
(BETH *exits.*)

HARRY

(*With controlled excitement*)
Boy, if this is true, it could knock the wedding right off the front page!

MARY

Gee, if they got Liz Livingstone's rocks, they got a million dollars!

HARRY

I hope they did! I need the story!

MARY

Me, too.
(*The bedroom door opens. A French* POLICE SERGEANT *and a* POLICEMAN *enter and cross the stage.*)

SERGEANT

Au voleur! Qui que sorte, abuse de notre hospitalité.

HARRY

What did they get?

}

Simultaneously

MARY

How did they get in?
(*The two* POLICEMEN *continue to converse in French.*)

HARRY

Hey, what happened? What happened?

SERGEANT

(*Stopping at the door*)
Parlez-vous français?

HARRY AND MARY

No!

SERGEANT

Quel dommage!
(*The* SERGEANT *and* POLICEMAN *exit.*)

HARRY

You—a society editor—can't speak French!

MARY

I can speak French but I can't understand it.
(BETH *enters with a red jacket over her arm.*)

MARY

Miss Livingstone!

HARRY

Listen, somebody's got to tell us something!
(*He takes hold of* BETH's *arm as* ARTURO *enters from the bedroom, right.*)

ARTURO

Who are these people?

BETH

Reporters.

ARTURO

Reporters! See here, as the manager of this hotel, I am taking a firm position in this matter. You are not to mention this robbery in the newspapers.

HARRY

You don't think we'd do a thing like that?

ARTURO

Good!
(*He starts for the door, left.*)

HARRY

Hey, wait a minute. What's the French law on this? Is the hotel responsible?

ARTURO

The hotel will be responsible up to the limit of our insurance —if we're insured.
(ARTURO *exits.*)

MARY

Miss Livingstone, please—what actually happened?

BETH

The burglar evidently came through the balcony window, but how he got out of the hotel in broad daylight with all our clothes, I'll never know.

HARRY

(*Desperate*)

Miss Livingstone, come clean—how much of your mother's jewelry was stolen?

BETH

Not a karat.

HARRY

(*Incredulous*)

How could anybody break in here and miss a million dollars' worth of jewels?

MARY

What did your mother do—hide them?

BETH

She did better than that—she slept in them.

> (LIZ *enters in pajamas which are covered with necklaces, brooches, clips and bracelets, set with diamonds, rubies, sapphires, emeralds.*)

LIZ

Hi—you newspaper people do get around, don't you?

HARRY

Wow! A walking Christmas tree.

31

LIZ

I made up my mind that if they were going to get my rocks, they'd have to take me, too. Up to now nobody's wanted this stuff at that price.

MARY

You mean all they got was some of your clothes?

BETH

Some of them? All of them!

LIZ

It's a good thing Beth was out riding. All I've got left is this pair of pajamas. I can't go anywhere in this.

HARRY

(*Taking a camera out of his pocket*)
Only on the front page of every newspaper in America! Hold it!

BETH

Mother, you can't be photographed that way.

LIZ

(*Surveying herself*)
I think this looks kinda cute. Go ahead and shoot.
(HARRY *snaps a few pictures.*)

MARY

Mrs. Livingstone, can you tell me exactly what clothes were stolen?

32

LIZ

There was a month's supply of evening gowns. . . .

MARY

How many would that be?

LIZ

Well, let's see, this is April—thirty! The hotel manager has a list of everything.

MARY

(*To* HARRY)

Let's go.
        (MARY *exits*.)

LIZ

Wait a minute! (HARRY *stops*) You've missed the point!

HARRY

What point?

LIZ

The whole story is this: With all our clothes stolen, we can't go to the wedding.

HARRY

Sorry, Mrs. Livingstone, that isn't much of a story.

LIZ

Not much of a story! Do you know what this means to a woman! Why—I—I—I could shoot myself!

HARRY

Now that would be a story.
(*He exits.* BETH *helps her mother into the red jacket.*)

LIZ

This is terrible. I don't know what the Kellys will think of us for not showing up.

BETH

(*An idea strikes her*)
Mother—we can go to the wedding.

LIZ

Huh?

BETH

Mrs. Waldron's just your size and she's got a terrific wardrobe.

LIZ

Baby, I wouldn't go without you.

BETH

Judy Heston's right on the next floor and she and I trade clothes at school all the time. (*She goes to the telephone*) We've got to hurry. I'll call Judy now.

LIZ

Baby—don't. (LIZ *opens her arms.* BETH *puts the receiver down and goes to her mother, who takes her in a close embrace.* LIZ's *face is toward the audience*) I've got something to tell you.
(*We hear* LIZ's *voice on a tape recording expressing her thoughts.*)

34

LIZ'S VOICE

Oh, Mr. Livingstone, how can I tell her? When you died I promised you that Beth would be in society—that she'd make the Main Line. And now what's happened? She's been snubbed by the Kellys! Well, Mr. Livingstone, I've just got to tell her the truth.

(BETH *pulls away from her mother.*)

LIZ

Baby, I've got a confession to make.

BETH

Mother, I think I know what's happened. We weren't invited to the wedding, were we?

LIZ

I'll make it up to you. I'll buy you something. I'll buy you a horse. You always feel better when I buy you a horse.

BETH

And just to save me from being hurt you went to all this trouble.

LIZ

What trouble?

BETH

You stole our clothes, didn't you?

LIZ

I know where they are. I can steal them back.

35

BETH

Mother, going to the wedding doesn't mean that much to me.
But I'm furious about their not inviting you.

LIZ

I'm used to it, baby. I've been taking it for years. But they
can't do this to my baby. I'll show them they can't!

BETH

Mother, you're wonderful!

LIZ

Baby, you're terrific!

BETH

You're everything they say you are—you're fabulous!

LIZ

You're not so unfabulous, yourself.

(*They sing, "Mutual Admiration Society"*)
We belong to a mutual admiration society

(LIZ)
My baby and me

(LIZ *and* BETH)
We belong to a mutual admiration society

(LIZ)
She thinks I'm beautiful and smart
I think that she's a work of art

(BETH)
She says that I am heaven-sent
And I'm her fan club president

(LIZ)
I tell her I'm so proud of her
She says that she is prouderer

(LIZ *and* BETH)
And that's the way
We pass the time of day

(LIZ)
My baby and me

(LIZ *and* BETH)
Oh, we belong to a mutual admiration society
We belong to a mutual admiration society

(LIZ)
My baby and me

(LIZ *and* BETH)
We belong to a mutual admiration society

(LIZ)
She says, "Oh, you're the sweetest one"
I say, "No, you're the sweetest one"

(BETH)

She claims that I'm a natural wit
I say it's just the opposite

(LIZ)

I think her singing is divine
She says it's not as good as mine

(LIZ *and* BETH)

And we go on
Like that from night 'til dawn
My baby and me
Oh, we belong to a mutual admiration society

(BETH)

I think she's absolutely great
She says that that's a family trait

(LIZ)

I say, "That kind of flattery
Will get you every place with me"

(LIZ *and* BETH)

The way we carry on it tends
To just embarrass all our friends
And that is how
We'll still be years from now
My baby and me
My baby and me

My baby and me!

(*At the end of the song there is a knock on the door, left.*)

LIZ

Who is it?

ARTURO

(*Off*)

It's me, madame! Arturo! Open quickly. I have news for you.

LIZ

N'est-ce pas!
(*There is another knock.*)

BETH

Entrez!

LIZ

Yeah—*entrez, n'est-ce pas.* That's what I was trying to think of.

(ARTURO *bursts into the room.*)

ARTURO

Madame, your wardrobe—your clothes which were stolen—they have been found—all of them—

LIZ

Well, that was sooner than I expected!

ARTURO

Everything you described, madame—and it is almost a joke —they were stuffed in the linen closet right across the hall.

39

LIZ

Well, think of that—(*To* BETH) It's a small world, isn't it?

ARTURO

And what's more, madame, we will catch the thief.

LIZ

Huh?

ARTURO

We have a witness. One of our guests. He saw the clothes being hidden.

LIZ

(*Worried*)

Arturo, I wouldn't prosecute . . .
(*There is a knock on the door.*)

ARTURO

Entrez! This is the witness.
(*The* DUKE OF GRANADA *opens the door and enters. He is a handsome, distinguished Spaniard, in his forties. He is dressed in the clothes of an automobile racer. He gives* BETH *a bow.*)

DUKE

Mademoiselle! (*He starts to bow to* LIZ) Mada—(*He stops and stares at her.* LIZ *turns away.*)

ARTURO

This is Madame Livingstone, the victim of the robbery. (*To* LIZ) Madame, may I present—

DUKE

(*Peremptorily*)

Arturo, tell my mechanic to wait for me!

(ARTURO *bows and leaves.* BETH *hurries to the bedroom door.*)

BETH

Mother, I'm sure you don't need—

LIZ

Beth, where are you going?

BETH

Just somewhere else.

(BETH *exits into the bedroom. The* DUKE *continues to look at* LIZ. *Gradually a smile breaks over his face.*)

DUKE

Madame, I came up here hoping to solve a mystery. Now I find I have discovered one.

LIZ

I'm not quite sure how to take that.

DUKE

Madame, why did you do it?

LIZ

Why did I do what?

DUKE

You stole your own clothes!

LIZ

What would I do a thing like that for?

DUKE

I saw you hide them! (LIZ *sits in a chair by the desk and hangs her head*) Ah, of course—I understand—you can't pay your bill—you don't want them to seize your clothes, so— Madame, if you are desperate for funds, I—(LIZ *rises, throws open her jacket and walks past him, flashing her jewels. He shields his eyes*) When you are passing someone you should dim your lights. This is something of which I must get to the bottom of.

LIZ

So I did it. You see, my daughter and I were expecting to be invited somewhere and we weren't. I didn't want her to be hurt.

DUKE

You must be a very nice person—and clever!
 (*The telephone rings.* LIZ, *her eyes on the* DUKE, *fumbles for it.*)

LIZ

I had to figure out some reason why we couldn't go. (*She has the telephone now and speaks into it*) Yes? . . . No, you must have the wrong room. . . . There's nobody like that here. . . . If there was a "His Majesty" around here wouldn't I know it?
 (THE DUKE *steps to her side and reaches for the receiver.*)

DUKE

Pardon—that must be for me.

LIZ

You?
(She doesn't quite believe it and holds onto the receiver, but he finally takes it.)

DUKE

(Into the telephone)
Sí, Carlos—tell him to wait. . . . Yes, I know what time the race is but they can hold it for me . . . Look, I am only ten minutes away. I can get there in five minutes.
(He hangs up. LIZ *walks around him, giving him a completely new appraisal.)*

LIZ

No kidding—are you a Majesty?

DUKE

I am addressed that way only by members of my household.

LIZ

Are you really a king or something?

DUKE

Not a reigning king.

LIZ

What other kinds are there?

DUKE

I am what is called a pretender.

LIZ

I like you all the better for admitting it.

43

DUKE

Admitting what?

LIZ

That you're a phony. It's very refreshing to meet one who comes clean about it. I admire you for it.

DUKE

(*Puzzled*)
Why do you say these things to me?

LIZ

Because—what did you call yourself?

DUKE

I am the Duke of Granada. I am the pretender to the throne of Spain. Do you know the difference between Bourbon and Hapsburg?

LIZ

Sure. One's whiskey and one's beer.

DUKE

Not in my country. You see, there are two royal families. Franco is supporting Prince Juan, the Bourbon pretender.

LIZ

Oh, and you're the Hapsburg pretender?

DUKE

Yes. I expect before too long I shall be king.

LIZ

So you're that kind of a pretender. Do you mind a personal question? (*He indicates he doesn't*) Is there a pretendress?

DUKE
(*Amused*)

There is no "pretendress."

LIZ

Oh, you're not married?

DUKE

No.

LIZ
(*Matter of factly*)

I'd like to have you meet my daughter.
    (*She starts for the bedroom door. He stops her.*)

DUKE

You mean that charming girl in riding clothes?

LIZ

That's the one. How about you two riding together tomorrow morning?

DUKE
(*Hesitating*)

Well—tomorrow morning—

LIZ

Good, it's a date. (*There is a knock on the door*) Come in, *n'est-ce pas.*
    (*The knock is repeated.*)

DUKE

Entrez!

    (LIZ *makes a gesture of annoyance with herself.* ARTURO *enters.*)

ARTURO

My deep apologies, Your Highness. But the race. . . . (*He points to his watch*) They will start without you.

DUKE

Arturo, flowers for madame!

ARTURO

A bouquet immediately, Your Highness.

DUKE

A bouquet? I said flowers . . . fill the suite with flowers!

ARTURO

Yes, Your Highness. (*Anxiously touching his watch again*) But, Your Highness . . . the race!

DUKE

    (*Dismissing him*)

They will wait.

ARTURO

    (*As he starts to go*)

I know you will win, Your Majesty, but please don't break your neck. (*He stumbles—but makes the door. To* LIZ) His Royal Highness can be very reckless.

    (*He goes.*)

LIZ

(*To the* DUKE, *concerned*)

Yeah. Be careful. You're too nice a guy to get hurt. (*She remembers*) And besides, you've got a date with my daughter tomorrow.

DUKE

Madame, *au revoir!*
    (*He bows.*)

LIZ

(*Bowing back*)

Entrez!

DUKE

(*This stops him, then he answers gallantly*)
N'est-ce pas!
    (*He exits.*)

LIZ

(*Calling*)

Beth! Beth!
    (*She makes the gesture currently used by teen-agers, shaking her hand as though to cool off her fingers after touching something that was too hot. Then we hear her thoughts on tape again.*)

LIZ'S VOICE

Mr. Livingstone, I may have a surprise for you. How would you like to be the future King of Spain's late father-in-law?
    (BETH *enters.*)

BETH

Well, when do you go to jail?

LIZ

We're not going to jail, but we *are* going some place. Beth, tell me. How does a Royal Highness stack up against a Serene Highness?

BETH

Mother, there is no Highness higher than a Royal Highness.

LIZ

That's all I wanted to know. Beth, we're going to out-Kelly the Kellys.

(LIZ *sings*)
My baby and me

(BETH *and* LIZ)
Oh, we belong to a mutual admiration society
Just between us two—four—six—eight
Oh, who do we appreciate?

(BETH)
Boy, when it starts it never stops
We just blow our respective tops

(LIZ *and* BETH)
The only fighting that we do
Is just who loves who more than who
And that is how

48

HAPPY HUNTING

We'll still be years from now
My baby and me
My baby and me
My baby and me.
  (*They exit.*)
        (*Blackout*)

Scene 3

A terrace outside the Hotel Riviera.
There are stairs upstage right, leading to the swimming pool at a higher elevation. Left is the entrance to the hotel. Onstage are several tables and chairs. At rise we see a group of girls in gay play clothes. After a moment, they sing, "For Love or Money."

(GIRLS)
There's nothin' we won't do for love or money
And if you want a honey lamb
You've got to really spread the jam
And we will spread the joy

We only have to see the moon or moola
And we start shoutin' "Oo-la-la"
And if we call you "Sweet Papa"
We ain't just bein' coy

Now man, we're all for makin' your eggs
That's if the bacon is there
And we know you know what we mean
Don't wanna be a stick in the mud
But when we're pickin' our friends
We like to pick 'em clean

Just tell us all that you have Dun and Bradstreet

50

That Bradstreet is a mad street, too
If you live there, well, we love you
You little honey bunny

We'll have a ball
We'll do it all
For love or money

So if you send a little note, endorse it
And Daddy-o, of course it will
Mean that we're just like Jack and Jill
Go fetch a pail of honey
We'll have a ball
We'll do it all
For love or money
Love or money
Or money
Money.

    (ARTURO *enters from the hotel, carrying under his arm
a large account book, glancing behind him nervously.
After a moment* SANDY *follows him on.*)

SANDY

Señor Arturo, why did you take away the account book? I
haven't finished with it yet.

ARTURO
(*Furtively*)
Mr. Stewart, do you mind examining it out here where my
wife will not see you?

SANDY

Señor Arturo, we are not questioning anyone's honesty. The syndicate my firm represents sent me here to find out why this hotel is losing so much money.

ARTURO

But that syndicate owns twenty-seven hotels. Certainly one of them can afford to lose money.

SANDY

Not this much money. (*He sits at a table and opens the account book*) There's one account here that's rather extraordinary. (*He refers to the book*) This Duke of Granada.

ARTURO

Oh, yes, Mr. Stewart. He is our most distinguished guest. He will some day be King of Spain. It is because of me that he stays in this hotel.

SANDY

Oh, I'm beginning to understand.

ARTURO

I'm Spanish, too, you know. In Spain I am the Baron de Cuavas. I am one of the Duke's chief supporters.

SANDY

(*Tapping the book*)
Yes, I noticed that. Could you arrange an appointment for me to see this Duke of Granada?

ARTURO

Well, he is royalty. He does not see everyone who asks.

SANDY

You know, Señor Arturo, I have to turn in a report on you, too.

ARTURO
(*Hastily*)

I shall arrange for an audience immediately. (*Starts out, then turns back*) Señor, my wife is very touchy about anyone looking at her account book. If she should come out here, don't let her see what you are doing.

SANDY

How will I know your wife?

ARTURO

She's short and fat and has a black moustache.
> (BETH *appears on the upper elevation and calls to* SANDY.)

BETH

Hello! (*He looks about but can't see anyone. She calls again*) Hello!
> (*This time he sees her.*)

SANDY

Hello! (BETH *comes down the stairs*) Where've you been? I had breakfast on the terrace this morning all alone. I know you didn't exactly promise—

BETH

I was out horseback riding.

SANDY

All by yourself?

BETH

(*Hoping to impress*)

No—no—with His Royal Highness.

SANDY

What royal highness?

BETH

The Duke of Granada.

SANDY

Oh, that one!

BETH

He's also the Prince of Hapsburg, the Count of—

SANDY

Yes, I know. The Count of Five Hundred and Sixty Four Million Francs. (*Pointing to the account book on table*) It's there in red ink.

BETH

What do you mean?

SANDY

That's how much he owes the hotel. He hasn't paid his bill for over a year.

BETH

All I know is, he's charming.

SANDY

Beth, I can't understand how a girl like you . . .

BETH

Don't be stuffy. Remember, I'm not a Main Liner.

SANDY

Your father was Main Line.

BETH

Yes, and soon as Father died, Mother and I were derailed.

SANDY

Well, Beth, your mother had a little trouble fitting in.

BETH

They never gave her a chance.

SANDY

Did she ever tell you about the hunt?

BETH

(Startled)

Mother at a hunt?

SANDY

(Nodding gravely)

The Unionville Hunt. (BETH *reacts with awe*) One week after your father brought her from Colorado.

BETH

(Almost afraid to ask)

What did she do?

55

SANDY

She turned up riding astride on a western saddle, dressed in Levis, and carrying a lariat. When the hunt started, she let out a wahoo, took off like a bat out of hell, and roped the fox.

BETH

That's why Mother won't get on a horse any more. But she loves to have me ride. She made the date for me with His Highness this morning. That's why I—wasn't around earlier.

SANDY

Oh, you don't have to explain to me.

BETH

But I'm free now. I'll even it up. I'll go swimming with you.

(*She takes a Bikini out of her pocket.*)

SANDY

Well, first I've got some work—(*He sees the Bikini*) What's that?

BETH

My bathing suit.

SANDY

You're not going to be seen in that?

BETH

Why not? Over here it's what they all wear.

56

SANDY

But you're from Philadelphia.

BETH

What difference does that make?

SANDY

But, I—I—haven't you any civic pride?

BETH

Yes, and I was planning to show it.
(SANDY, *in his nervousness, has picked up a beach ball from a nearby chair.* BETH *takes it from him and goes into a dance, using the ball as part of the dance. At the end of the dance she starts off.*)

SANDY

(*Calling after her*)

Beth! You are not to put that on. I'm asking you in the name of William Penn!

(*Blackout*)

Scene 4

The verandah of the DUKE's *suite at the Hotel Riviera.*

The doorway leading to the DUKE's *suite is stage left. Across the verandah, stage right, we see the portico of* LIZ LIVING-STONE's *suite.*

At rise, a WAITER *is just finishing setting a small table, stage center, for breakfast.* COUNT CARLOS IBAÑEZ, *the* DUKE's *Lord Chamberlain, enters from the* DUKE's *suite and surveys the table. What he sees obviously displeases him and he speaks sharply to the* WAITER.

COUNT CARLOS

How many times have I given orders that His Royal Highness is never to be served on hotel china?

WAITER

I'm new here.

COUNT CARLOS

Inside you will find His Majesty's gold service.
(ARTURO *enters from the* DUKE's *suite, the* WAITER *passing him as he exits.*)

ARTURO

Good morning, Count Carlos.

58

COUNT CARLOS

(*Taking a paper from his pocket*)
Arturo, as His Highness's Lord Chamberlain, I must protest.
I found in his mail this morning this bill for the repair of his
airplane, with a rather nasty note. Why hasn't the hotel taken
care of this?
(*The* WAITER *returns with the gold service.*)

ARTURO

Well, the Duke's bills have been so high—

COUNT CARLOS

Pay it immediately. (*He hands the bill to* ARTURO) The
Duke may be without money, but we cannot have his credit
impaired.

ARTURO

But with everything—his racing cars, his speed boats, his
stable, his stamp collection—being charged to the hotel it's
beginning to look bad on the books.

COUNT CARLOS

But what can happen? You are the manager of this hotel.
(*The* WAITER *has finished setting the gold service, and
exits.*)

ARTURO

What can happen? It has happened. A young lawyer from
America examined the books today and now he has asked me
for an audience with His Highness.

COUNT CARLOS

Keep him away—by all means, keep him away.
(*The* DUKE *has entered and overhears this.*)

DUKE

Keep who away?

ARTURO

It is nothing. Just a young American who was eager to meet Your Highness.

DUKE

Good. Invite him to come in.

COUNT CARLOS

But, Your Highness . . .

DUKE

(*To* ARTURO)

I shall receive him.

ARTURO

Yes, Your Highness. If that is your pleasure.
(ARTURO *exits. The* DUKE *sits down to his breakfast.*)

DUKE

Carlos, I find Americans fascinating. Did you know they wear diamonds on their pajamas.
(ARTURO *returns with* SANDY, *who is carrying an attaché case.* ARTURO *straightens* SANDY'S *coat and motions to him to straighten his tie. As* SANDY *does so, he drops his attaché case.* ARTURO *quickly picks it up and hands it to* SANDY.)

ARTURO

Your Highness, Mr. Sanford Stewart. (*The* DUKE *turns*) Mr. Stewart, His Royal Highness, the Prince of Hapsburg, Duke of Granada.

SANDY

(*Bowing*)

Your Highness!

DUKE

Hi! I believe that's the official American greeting.

SANDY

Yes, and, Your Highness, I happen to be here on official business. (*He sits*) Your Highness, my law firm represents the syndicate that owns this hotel.

DUKE

Oh! Then you must stay here as my guest.

SANDY

How kind of you.
    (SANDY *sits. He jiggles nervously on the chair. The* DUKE *puts a calming hand on his shoulder.*)

DUKE

Will you join me for breakfast? This is something very special—oranges and limes grown only in Valencia. Arturo has them flown in for me fresh every morning.

SANDY

Has them flown in? Just for you? Isn't that very expensive?

61

DUKE

I don't find it so. The service here is excellent—thanks to Arturo.

ARTURO

(*Nervously*)

If Your Highness will excuse me—
    (ARTURO *exits*.)

SANDY

Your Highness, I asked for this audience because I have been examining the accounts and it appears that the amount of Your Highness's unpaid bills is identical with the hotel's losses.

DUKE

Isn't that a coincidence!

SANDY

Yes, I thought so myself! (*The* DUKE *laughs and* SANDY *joins him in the laugh*) So my firm sent me here to do something about it.

DUKE

Good! Good!

COUNT CARLOS

His Highness might be interested in knowing what you are going to do about it.

DUKE

Yes, this is too good a hotel to let run at a loss.

SANDY

I'm glad you feel that way. Therefore, I must inform you that you must pay your bill or leave the hotel.

DUKE

(*Firmly*)

The audience is over!

SANDY

(*Rising*)

As of now, we are cutting off Your Highness's credit.

DUKE

Young man, you have finally succeeded in offending me.

SANDY

This account must be settled no later than Thursday.

DUKE

You will have my check in the morning.

SANDY

Yes, but the bill must be paid by Thursday.
(SANDY *exits.*)

DUKE

Carlos, why haven't you paid this bill?

COUNT CARLOS

But how, Your Majesty?

DUKE

With money—(*He rises*) my income from Spain—from the Hapsburgs—from the Royalist Party—(*He sees that* CARLOS *is shaking his head*) Isn't there any?

COUNT CARLOS

Your Majesty, Arturo and I did not want you to know—but for more than a year there has been no income.

DUKE

Have you called this to the attention of my supporters?

COUNT CARLOS

They have called it to my attention. When you won the thousand kilometer race, they wrote asking whether you could send them money—part of the purse.

DUKE

My supporters?

COUNT CARLOS

Yes.

DUKE

Who's supporting who? (*He turns*) I shouldn't have said that. They have been very loyal and generous. I must find some way to repay them. But how, I do not know.
(LIZ *enters on her portico.*)

LIZ

Hi, Duke!
(*He turns and sees her.*)

DUKE

Madame!

LIZ

You've got a beautiful day for pretending.

DUKE

As a matter of fact, not very. Mrs. Livingstone, tell me something—How do people who haven't got money get money?

LIZ

How do they get it? They work.

DUKE

(*To* COUNT CARLOS)

Carlos, we're in trouble. (*He pauses*) One of us has to think of something. You start first.

(COUNT CARLOS *bows and exits.*)

LIZ

(*Joining the* DUKE)

I hear you won the race yesterday. Congratulations.

DUKE

Thank you.

LIZ

I also hear you had a narrow escape.

DUKE

It was very close. You see, to win I had to pass this car or go over him.

LIZ

Which did you do?

DUKE

(*Gestures*)

He hit a bump—(*Also with a gesture*) and I went under him.

LIZ

Yeah, you're famous for taking chances. I've been talking to people about you. According to my personal Gallup Poll, you're nuts.

DUKE

Nuts?
(*She sits at the table.*)

LIZ

You know—just a little screwy. Horse races, speed boat races, automobiles, airplanes—and on quiet days, skin-diving and ski-jumping. What are you trying to do, kill yourself?

DUKE

Au contraire, madame—I am trying not to kill myself.

LIZ

You seem to come pretty close to it.

DUKE

Of course, that is the whole idea. You don't know how good it is to be alive until you almost lose your life.

LIZ

To me that sounds kinda dangerous.

DUKE

Madame, you love comfort, don't you?

LIZ

Yeah—and plenty of it.

66

DUKE

Well—I love danger. It's exciting . . . it's exhilarating . . .
it becomes irresistible.

(He sings, "It's Like a Beautiful Woman")
It's like a beautiful woman
You know is wrong for you
But you can't get her out of your system
You just can't leave her alone
It's like a beautiful woman
Who spells bad news for you
But you're hopelessly caught in her clutches
And you can't call your soul your own
You make up your mind
Once and for all
You're going to call it quits
And you try to call it quits
You try your damnedest to
I really do
But I know I'm only human
And when she smiles at me
Then I forget all the wickedness I know she's capable of
It's like a beautiful woman
You can't help but love.

LIZ

Well, that's a switch. I've heard of people flirting with
danger but you're in love with it. Don't you think it would be
more sensible if—

DUKE

I know what you're going to say. Yes, I've thought about

leading a quiet life—you know—twenty-five miles an hour—
safety belts—

(*He goes back into the song*)
But I know I'm only human
And when she smiles at me
Then I forget all the wickedness I know she's capable of
It's like a beautiful woman
You can't help but love.

LIZ

Do you know what else is like a beautiful woman?

DUKE

What?

LIZ

A beautiful woman.

DUKE

In your presence, madame, who would not think so?

LIZ

Oh, you'd go over great in America.

DUKE

Me? In America?

LIZ

I don't quite know how to do the Emily Post bit on this,
but—(*She rises*) Mrs. Elizabeth Livingstone requests the pleasure of His Royal Highness's presence at her home in Philadelphia for as long as His Royal Highness wants to stay as
her Royal Guest—R.S.V.P. Answer right away, *n'est-ce pas.*

DUKE

(*Looks hesitant*)

But, madame . . .

LIZ

The whole thing is on the cuff.

DUKE

I have been at this hotel a long, long time. I feel I owe them something.

LIZ

That can be taken care of. (*He gives her a look*) You'll be just as comfortable in my home. I've got a house as big as this place.

DUKE

There are my horses.

LIZ

Bring 'em along. They can visit our horses. I've got lots of horses.

DUKE

I have my entourage.

LIZ

You won't need it. I've got four Cadillacs.

DUKE

I mean my staff.

LIZ

There'll be room. I always have two or three suites reserved on a boat.

DUKE

You must be very wealthy.

LIZ

I'm filthy. My husband left me four million and I ran it up to forty million.

DUKE

Dollars?

LIZ

What do you think—asparagus tips?
(*He studies her for a moment.*)

DUKE

Madame, may I ask one question? What's behind all this?

LIZ

Well, my daughter is—well, my daughter—that's it in a nutshell.

DUKE

Madame, are you suggesting that I would marry for money?

LIZ

Well, now, Duke—

DUKE

Because if you're not—I'm not interested.

LIZ

You mean if I were, you would?

DUKE

If you are—I am.

LIZ

(*Extending her hand*)

Slip me your duke, Duke—we're in business.

(*Blackout*)

The quay.
The backdrop is the side of a gigantic ocean liner. At stage left is a gangplank.
There is the usual just-before-sailing rush. Porters are carrying luggage aboard, passengers are presenting their tickets to a SHIP'S OFFICER *at a small desk at the foot of the gangplank. There are small groups, friends saying good-byes to other friends about to sail. At far right is a young couple locked in an embrace and kiss.* MRS. STEWART *and* SANDY *enter.*

MRS. STEWART

Sanford, did you know that those Livingstones were going to be on this ship?

SANDY

Mother, Beth Livingstone's a very nice girl and I want you to meet her.
(*He goes to the desk with their tickets.* HARRY WATSON *enters.*)

HARRY

I beg your pardon. I represent the Chicago *Tribune*. You're Mrs. Sanford Stewart of Philadelphia, aren't you?
(*He holds out his hand.*)

MRS. STEWART

I don't see how that could possibly be of interest to anyone in Chicago.

> *(She exits up the gangplank.* SANDY *starts to follow her, sees* HARRY'S *outstretched hand, shakes it, then exits.* ARTURO *enters, takes his tickets to the* SHIP'S OFFICER.)

SHIP'S OFFICER

Hello, Arturo.

ARTURO

Please, you will address me as the Baron de Cuavas. I am now in the service of His Royal Highness.

SHIP'S OFFICER

The hotel will miss you.

ARTURO

I do not stay where I am not wanted, especially after I have been told to get out.

> *(The* DUKE *enters.)*

DUKE

Arturo, I am looking forward to this adventure, aren't you?

ARTURO

I am so grateful His Highness is taking me with him.

DUKE

After what that Mr. Stewart did to you because of me, it was the least I could do. I am sorry we couldn't take your wife.

73

ARTURO

(Bowing)

I am grateful for that, too.

DUKE

You will be very useful to me, Baron. Once on board you will devote yourself to the marriage contract.

ARTURO

I will start negotiations with Mrs. Livingstone immediately.

DUKE

I want everything settled before we reach America.
(The SHIP'S OFFICER *returns the tickets to* ARTURO.*)*

SHIP'S OFFICER

You may go aboard.

ARTURO

If it does not work out, I could approach the United States Government. They are lending money to Franco.

DUKE

I am under the impression Mrs. Livingstone has more money than the United States Government.
(They exit up the gangplank. LIZ *enters and rushes to the* SHIP'S OFFICER.*)*

LIZ

Has my daughter gone aboard yet? Beth Livingstone?

74

SHIP'S OFFICER

I'll look at the list.
(*He consults his list.* LIZ *goes to the kissing couple and separates them.*)

LIZ

I'm sorry. My mistake. I'm looking for my daughter. (*There is a short blast from the ship's whistle.* LIZ *pushes the couple back into their embrace*) Go back to work. You've only got a minute.
(*The couple exit left. Passengers, among them the reporters and photographers who have covered the wedding, drift on during the scene.*)

SHIP'S OFFICER

Your daughter's not on board, Mrs. Livingstone.

MAUD

(*Entering with* BETH)
Liz, here she is. She was looking for Sandy Stewart.

BETH

He and his mother are sailing with us.

LIZ

Never mind them. You get on board and find our guest—and be very nice to him.

BETH

Are you throwing me at the Duke?

75

LIZ

Yeah—and you see that it isn't a wild pitch.
(*She pushes* BETH *up the gangplank.*)

MAUD

I'll wait for the tickets, Liz. You go find a good spot on deck. They tell me we're going to pass right by the royal yacht.

LIZ

I hope we do. When I was ten years old my father taught me to spit through my teeth.
> (LIZ *exits up the gangplank.* MAUD *moves over to the* SHIP'S OFFICER'S *desk and starts to look in her handbag for her tickets. There is a blast from the whistle and the reporters and photographers form a line behind* MAUD.)

MAUD

I won't be a minute, fellows. (*She continues to dig into her bag*) I'm as anxious to get out of here as you newspaper people are. (*She finds the tickets*) Oh, here they are!
(*She hands them to the* SHIP'S OFFICER.)

JACK

Well, Harry, we're about to leave little old Monaco.

HARRY

I can hardly wait.
> (*The passengers, reporters and photographers sing, "Wedding-of-the-Year Blues"*)

HAPPY HUNTING

(BOYS)
We're up to here
With the wedding of the year
Up to here with the wedding of the year

(FIRST BOY)
I am fatigued

(SECOND BOY)
Beat

(THIRD BOY)
Bushed

(FOURTH BOY)
Pooped

(FIFTH BOY)
Dead

(FIRST GIRL)
I'd like to spend

(SECOND GIRL)
A

(THIRD GIRL)
Week

(FOURTH GIRL)
In

(FIFTH GIRL)
Bed

(GIRLS)

Marriage

(ALL)

Marriage
Give me a nice juicy messy divorce

(TWO GIRLS)

Fed up with the phantasmagoria
Very unhappy with the spirit of euphoria

(HARRY)

I don't want to write another word about
Preparations
Into which everything but the kitchen sink went
Just give me a good old, one-hundred-percent,
Red-blooded, American
Juvenile delinquent.

(BOYS)

We're up to here
With the wedding of the year
Up to here with the wedding, up to here.

(FIRST BOY)

If I see another glass of pink champagne, I'm gonna brain
somebody

(FIRST GIRL)

If I see any more dancing in the streets, I'm gonna
call a cop

(SECOND BOY)

If I hear one more word about joy reigning supreme,
  I'll scream

(TWO GIRLS)

If there is one more jewel theft
There won't be one more jewel left

(SECOND GIRL)

I've had it with the cheering and the laughter
If I never hear about another fairy tale romance
I can live happily ever after

(THIRD GIRL)

It looked like a wrestling bout

(MAUD)

And I say let's get the hell out.
  (MAUD *exits up the gangplank*.)

(ALL)

We're up to here
With the wedding of the year
Uptial here with the nuptial of the year

(THIRD BOY)

All that regal rigmarole, you may love it
But as far as I'm concerned, you can take it and . . .
  (*The* FIFTH BOY *pokes him before he can finish.*)

(ALL)

We're up to here
With the wedding of the year

79

Up to, we're
Up to here
Up to, clear
Up to, we're
Up to here!

(*Blackout*)

SCENE 6

The ship's bar.
We see first the afterdeck of the ocean liner on its way to the United States, and an upper deck with a smokestack, stairs on either side leading to the lower deck. It is on this deck that we find the bar—a small enclosure with chairs and tables. The bar moves forward, to give the scene intimacy, as MAUD *and* LIZ *enter and the action begins.*

MAUD

Liz, this is the most thrilling thing I've ever heard!

LIZ

Take it easy—the deal isn't signed yet.
(*They have reached a table with two chairs, and they sit.*)

MAUD

If anybody can put this over, it's you. Beth's going to be Queen of Spain, I can feel it in my bones.

LIZ

Don't spread it around. I want to be the one to tell Margaret Kelly.

MAUD

I just can't wait to meet the Duke.
(ARTURO *enters and bows.*)

ARTURO

Madame, His Highness sends his compliments. He will join you directly.

(MAUD *pokes* LIZ.)

LIZ

Thank you. I'd like you to meet Mrs. Foley.

ARTURO

(*To* MAUD)

Madame!

(MAUD *starts to stand up.* LIZ *stops her.*)

LIZ

Sit down, he's only a baron.

ARTURO

Madame, there was something I wanted to take up with you.

LIZ

Okay. Shoot.

ARTURO

It's just that—I am eager to resume our conversations—our negotiations.

LIZ

Oh, yes. Well, there's a young man on board who works for my firm of lawyers. I'm going to turn the whole thing over to him. His name is Stewart . . . Sanford Stewart.

ARTURO

(*Stiffening*)

Sanford Stewart? I have met him. With me he is *persona non grata.*

LIZ

Fine! I'll tell him to get in touch with you.

ARTURO

If you insist, madame. (*He bows and starts to exit. The* DUKE *enters*) Your Highness, madame is waiting.
  (*He goes. The* DUKE *sees* LIZ *and* MAUD *and goes to their table.*)

DUKE

May I join you?
  (LIZ *and* MAUD *rise.*)

LIZ

Your Highness, may I present my friend, Maud Foley.
  (MAUD *drops a low, full, formal curtsy.*)

LIZ

  (*Staring at the prostrate* MAUD)
Eight to five she can't get up.
  (*As a matter of fact,* MAUD *can't get up. The* DUKE *extends his hand and helps her.*)

DUKE

  (*To* MAUD)
Madame, that is not necessary.

MAUD

  (*Rising*)
This is a great pleasure, Your Highness.

LIZ

  (*Addressing* MAUD, *trying to sound very casual*)
Scram.

MAUD

(*Continuing to address the* DUKE)

You know, I was just saying to Mrs. Livingstone that . . .

LIZ

(*A bit firmer*)

Scram.

MAUD

I was just saying I'll scram.
(*She backs out. A* BARMAN *enters and stands expectant.*)

LIZ

(*To the* DUKE)

Will you have a snort?

DUKE

(*A little hesitant*)

A snort? Yes. You?

LIZ

Sure.

DUKE

(*Signaling to the* BARMAN)

Two snorts.
(*The* BARMAN *shrugs and goes. The* DUKE *sits.*)

LIZ

Haven't seen you all afternoon.

DUKE

I've been playing deck tennis with Beth.

LIZ
(*Elaborately casual*)
Oh, you call her Beth now?

DUKE
Yes, we're getting along famously.

LIZ
(*Wistfully*)
That's swell—Your Highness.

DUKE
We should be with first names, too. May we not—Leez?
(LIZ *lights up.*)

LIZ
Hi—Jamie!
(*The* DUKE *looks around to see whom she is addressing, then turns back to her.*)

DUKE
Who is Jamie?

LIZ
That's you.

DUKE
Me?

LIZ
I've seen your name in the papers—J-a-i-m-e.

DUKE
In Spanish that is pronounced Hymie.

85

LIZ

J-A-I-M-E? That's a hell of a way to spell Hymie. What will your name be when you get to be King?

DUKE

I shall be King Jaime the First.

LIZ

You'll be the first Hymie that ever was a king. I can't wait until Philadelphia gets a load of you. Hymie, you'll fracture them. You're my answer to the Main Line.

DUKE

The Main Line?

LIZ

That's the royalty of Philadelphia.

DUKE

Philadelphia has royalty?

LIZ

Self-appointed royalty.

DUKE

Well, Napoleon crowned himself. You are part of this Main Line?

LIZ

They won't even speak to me.

DUKE

How could they not accept you—you, with your color, your personality, your wealth—

LIZ

I'll say this for the Main Line. You can't buy your way into
it. Me, I did the worst thing you could possibly do. I married
into it.

DUKE

Then you are not of Philadelphia?

LIZ

I'm from Colorado.

DUKE

Now you are talking my language. Colorado is Spanish.

LIZ

Gee, Hymie, I didn't know I knew any Spanish.

DUKE

Colorado means red.

LIZ

Not now—now it's Republican. We lived up in the moun-
tains—my paw and me. I don't remember my mother. My paw
was what we call a character. His name was Jones—"If'n"
Jones.

DUKE

"If'n"? You mean Ivan.

LIZ

No, I mean "If'n." It was a nickname. He'd never say anything positively. He'd say: "We'll get a bear tomorrow if'n we
can pick up some tracks." "We'll catch us some trout this week,
if'n they're where they were this time last year."

DUKE

Ah! That is where you get that openness of spirit. You were brought up in the outdoors.

LIZ

Yeah—paw was a hunter—and when we needed cash money he acted as a guide. That's how I met Mr. Livingstone—Beth's father. He came out from Philadelphia on a fishing trip.

DUKE

And he caught you.

LIZ

It was an accident—in a way. You see, Mr. Livingstone broke his leg. Paw carried him back to our cabin and it was up to me to nurse him. I was only sixteen then but I was well developed.

DUKE

You were smart for your age, eh?

LIZ

No—I was (*With a half-gesture*)—well developed.

DUKE

(*Mistaking the gesture*)

Ah—strong, eh?

LIZ

(*With desperate impatience*)

I was well stacked!

DUKE

Ah—*estaba buena! Cara, estaba redonda—fogosa.*
(*He laughingly rattles off a line of Spanish to indicate that he understands.*)

LIZ

I'm not sure what you're saying but I think you've caught on.
Anyway we put Mr. Livingstone in Paw's bed and then I . . .

DUKE

I know—I've seen that movie—You were a wonderful nurse—
and he got well.

LIZ

As a matter of fact, he got worse. One morning Paw said,
"I'm going down the mountain and I'll bring back Doc
Baker tomorrow, if'n it don't snow."

DUKE

Yes?

LIZ

It snowed. It snowed for three days. I couldn't get out of
the cabin to the woodpile. I had to keep Mr. Livingstone
warm. I burned all the chairs. I burned all the tables. Finally
I even burned my own bed.

DUKE

Then what did you do?
(*There is a momentary silence.* LIZ *looks a trifle em-
barrassed and then she finally blurts out in her own
defense.*)

LIZ

Well, you can't let a man freeze to death.

DUKE

No, that would be inhuman.

LIZ

I think I ought to tell you that Mr. Livingstone was a gentle-man. Very nice and very shy. All Philadelphia men are shy. I think it's the water. Anyway, when Paw finally got back with Doc Baker, it just happened that Mr. Livingstone and I were both asleep. Paw came over and cleared his throat and we woke up. Paw said, "Doc Baker here is also a justice of the peace, if'n we need a justice of the peace."

DUKE

And so you were married?

LIZ

Right then and there. You see, I didn't want to tell Paw in front of Doc Baker there was really no call for a justice of the peace. And Mr. Livingstone—

DUKE

(*Nodding*)

He was a gentleman.

LIZ

Oh, he really was! I could tell that the first time I met him.
(*She sings, "Mr. Livingstone."*)
Mr. Livingstone was a gent
From his fingertips to his toes
There I stood lookin' up at him
There he stood lookin' down his nose
He said, "How ja do?
How are you?"
I said to my future groom,
"Mr. Livingstone, I presume"

HAPPY HUNTING

Mr. Livingstone, Mr. Livingstone, Mr. Livingstone
He was every inch a gentleman

Even during our honeymoon
He continued to be polite
Just as proper as he could be
Then a year from our wedding night
Came a little tap,
Tiny rap
On the door of my bedroom
Mr. Livingstone, I presume

Mr. Livingstone, Mr. Livingstone, Mr. Livingstone
He was every inch a gentleman

Well, he gave me my first champagne
And the ceiling began to swing
And I had me some more champagne
And I can't recall one damn thing!
Oh, I only know
Later, though
That I had a little bloom
Mr. Livingstone's, I presume

Mr. Livingstone, Mr. Livingstone, Mr. Livingstone
He was every inch a gentleman

Mr. Livingstone was a gent
Right on up to his dying day
So I never did have much fun
And I guess it'll stay that way
With my luck so far

Chances are
They will carve upon my tomb
"Mrs. Livingstone, we presume"

Mr. Livingstone, Mr. Livingstone, Mr. Livingstone
He was every inch a gentleman

If I mind all my P's and Q's
Up to heaven I'll go one day
With a little harp in my hand
And a map of the milky way
Who'll be in the crowd
On a cloud
When St. Peter's portals loom?
Mr. Livingstone, I presume

Mr. Livingstone, Mr. Livingstone, Mr. Livingstone
He was every inch a gentleman.

(*Blackout*)

Scene 7

The afterdeck of the ship. This scene takes place some time later on in the voyage and the passengers look gayer. They are dressed more casually. A lot of them are sitting around on deck chairs. Among the passengers is a group of five college boys with musical instruments. They are noodling away. BETH *is listening with great enjoyment.* SANDY *enters, obviously looking for someone. He sees* BETH, *goes up to her, takes her by the arm and leads her down to a corner away from the group, where he can talk to her alone.*

BETH

What's the matter? What do you want?

SANDY

What do I want? I want to know what's going on.

BETH

We're just kidding around. You know, these boys played at the wedding party.

SANDY

I don't mean this—I mean your mother.

BETH

What's happened to Mother?

SANDY

It's happened to me!

93

BETH

What?

SANDY

(*Looking over his shoulder*)

Well, it's not proper for me to discuss a client's business—
but your mother has ordered me to negotiate a marriage settle-
ment between you and this—this—Duke.

BETH

(*Needling*)

Well, if'n she told you to do it, why aren't you doing it?

SANDY

I have been doing it. I have been sitting there for hours
with that Baron, and what I was planning to do this afternoon
was to have you meet my mother.

BETH

(*Coolly*)

Was she planning to meet me?

SANDY

(*Overprotesting*)

Mother will love you and you will love her. She's so . . .

BETH

Well, if'n we get along . . .

SANDY

(*Quickly*)

Don't say "if'n" in front of Mother. It'll upset her. Now,
Beth, about this Duke business. . . . You know how I feel
about you.

BETH

No, I don't.

SANDY

Beth, you can't expect me to put it into words. But I will tell you this: I can't let you marry a bankrupt Hapsburg.

BETH

Why not? He wants to marry me.

SANDY

Well, maybe somebody else might want to marry you.

BETH

If'n they did, they would have to come right out and ask me. (*Somewhere along here the college boys are playing very softly, setting the beat of the song that will follow.*)

SANDY

Beth, if'n you got to be a duchess, you'd have to stop saying "if'n."

BETH

Then I just won't be a duchess. I inherited "if'n" from my grandfather.

SANDY

Was your grandfather a lawyer?

BETH

No.

SANDY

He should have been. If'n—that's good—You can mean what you say without saying what you mean.
(*He sings, "If'n"*)

95

If'n I say I love you, baby
If'n I say I do
If'n I say that
Say that I say that
If'n I do
Only if'n I do
Would you say right back to me, I love you too?

If'n I was to kiss you, mind you
If'n I happen to
If'n I do that
Say that I do that
If'n I do
Even if'n I do
Would you cuddle up to me, and kiss me too?

If'n I got up the gumption, baby
If'n I sweetheart you good
If'n I was to fall
Of which there ain't much likelihood

But just say
If'n I say I love you, baby
If'n I say I do
If'n I say that
Say that I say that
If'n I do
Only if'n I do
Would you say right back to me, I love you too?
If'n I do
If'n I do
If'n I do
Only if'n I do.
If'n I say I love you, baby

(BETH)

If'n I say I love you

(SANDY)

If'n I say I do

(BETH)

If'n I say I do

(SANDY *and* BETH)

If'n I say that
Say that I say that
If'n I do
Only if'n I do

(SANDY)

Would you say right back to me, I love you too?
If'n I was to kiss you, mind you

(BETH)

If'n I was to kiss you

(SANDY)

If'n I happen to

(BETH)

If'n I happen to

(SANDY *and* BETH)

If'n I do that
Say that I do that
If'n I do
Even if'n I do

(SANDY)

Would you cuddle up to me, and kiss me too?

If'n I got up the gumption, baby
If'n I was so inclined
If'n I lost my heart
Which is the last thing in my mind

But just say
If'n I say I love you, baby

(BETH)
If'n I say I love you

(SANDY)
If'n I say I do

(BETH)
If'n I say I do

(SANDY *and* BETH)
If'n I say that
Well, just supposin'
If'n I do

(SANDY)
Assumin' if'n I do
Would you say right back to me, I love you too?

(SANDY *and* BETH)
Would you say right back to me, I love you too?
If'n I do
If'n I do
If'n I do
Only if'n I do!

(*Blackout*)

SCENE 8

The bar of the ship again.
MRS. SANFORD STEWART, SR., *is seated at a table, in evening dress, sipping a cocktail and reading a book. She is wearing glasses.* MAUD FOLEY, *leafing through a magazine, is sitting at the next table, also in evening dress, studying* MRS. STEWART. MRS. STEWART *puts down her book and sips her cocktail.* MAUD *takes advantage of this opportunity.*

MAUD

It's been a very smooth crossing so far, hasn't it? (MRS. STEWART *gives her a brief smile and nod and goes back to her book again*) That must be an interesting book you're reading, Mrs. Stewart. What's the name of it?
(*This time* MRS. STEWART *takes her glasses off and looks* MAUD *squarely in the eye.*)

MRS. STEWART

I don't believe I know you.

MAUD

I'm Mrs. T. Joseph Foley.

MRS. STEWART

I was right. I don't know you.
(*She goes back to her book.* SANDY *enters with* BETH *and sees his mother.*)

99

SANDY

Mother, I want you to meet Beth Livingstone.

BETH

How do you do, Mrs. Stewart?
(MRS. STEWART *nods in acknowledgment.*)

MRS. STEWART

Sanford, you haven't changed for dinner yet. Shouldn't you be starting?

SANDY

Mother, remember I told you about Miss Livingstone. You know how eager you were to meet her.
(MRS. STEWART *gives* BETH *a hasty glance.*)

MRS. STEWART

I think the young lady should be changing, too.

SANDY

(*He is desperately trying to warm up the proceedings*)
You've seen Miss Livingstone ride in the Devon Horse Show—Remember? (*There is no comment*) Well, since Nancy won't be home to show our horses this year, I thought it would be wonderful to have Miss Livingstone show them.

MRS. STEWART

Sanford, I have been meaning to tell you . . .

SANDY

(*Going right on*)
. . . And she could stay at our place the week of the show.

MRS. STEWART

Sanford, we are not showing at Devon this year.

SANDY

(*Puzzled*)

Oh, we're not? Well, Miss Livingstone could stay with us for the show anyway.

MRS. STEWART

The house will be closed that week.

SANDY

Mother—why?

MRS. STEWART

I've decided to go to Bar Harbor early this year.

BETH

(*Pleasantly but firmly*)

Mrs. Stewart, please overlook Sandy's invitation if'n it's going to cause you that much trouble.

MRS. STEWART

I'm sorry Sanford didn't know about my plans. (LIZ *enters, and stands in the back.* MRS. STEWART *turns to* SANDY) I'll go ahead, dear. Please dress for dinner immediately.

(*She exits with her book, but leaves her glasses on the table.* LIZ *watches her leave.*)

LIZ

I think we just passed an iceberg. (*To* BETH, *who is looking grim*) Well, Beth, I tried to tell you. Those Main Line trains can run right over you.

MAUD

I'll say they can. Liz, you should have heard.

(MAUD *tosses the magazine on the table, covering* MRS. STEWART's *glasses*.)

SANDY

Beth, I'm sorry about this. Give me a chance to talk to Mother.

(MRS. STEWART *returns*.)

MRS. STEWART

I left my glasses somewhere. (*To* SANDY) Sanford, look around for my glasses. (*To* MAUD) Have you seen my glasses?

MAUD

(*Her big moment has arrived*)
I don't believe I know you.

MRS. STEWART

I beg your pardon?

MAUD

I said, I don't believe I know you.

MRS. STEWART

(*Casually and very simply*)
I wouldn't permit you to know me. (*Then, as* SANDY *finds her glasses and hands them to her*) Thank you, Sandy.

(*She exits.* MAUD *stares after her, open-mouthed.* LIZ *speaks with admiration.*)

LIZ

(*To* MAUD)
They've got something! Damn it, you've got to admit, they've got something!

BETH

Something I don't happen to like.

SANDY

Beth, she's my mother. You may not like what she represents, but—

LIZ

That reminds me, I thought you represented me. (SANDY *turns toward her inquiringly*) You and the Baron were supposed to get together on that marriage contract. He tells me you won't get down to business.

SANDY

Mrs. Livingstone, I can't take that seriously.

LIZ

Why not?

SANDY

Because Beth isn't taking it seriously.

BETH

(*To* SANDY)

I'm taking it very seriously. Please finish the contract—and make it foolproof. I'm dressing for dinner, Mother.
(*She exits.* SANDY *looks after her for a minute, then turns to* LIZ. *He is now all business.*)

SANDY

I think I should tell you, Mrs. Livingstone, the Baron's demands have been so high that, as your attorney . . .

LIZ

You settle on their terms.

SANDY

Well, Mrs. Livingstone (*Hesitating*) In our discussions—I feel I must tell you—there are other obstacles. And I—

LIZ

(*Cutting in*)
Settle on their terms. Those are my orders.

SANDY

Very well.
(*He bows and exits.*)

LIZ

Maud, I've got to have a drink. (*She calls off*) Hey, Louie!

MAUD

You've got to have a drink! (*The* BARMAN *enters*) I want a double Scotch and some Band-aids.

LIZ

I'll have a Manhattan—only make it with gin instead of whiskey—(*The* BARMAN *starts out. She stops him*) and put an olive in it instead of a cherry—aw, hell, you might as well make me a martini.
(*The* BARMAN *exits.* LIZ *sits at a table thoughtfully.* MAUD *joins her.*)

MAUD

What are you so quiet about?

LIZ

Those obstacles he mentioned. I wish I'd asked him what they were.

MAUD

He didn't seem to want to discuss them. So it seems fairly obvious . . .

LIZ

What's obvious?

MAUD

Liz . . .

LIZ

What's obvious?

MAUD

Liz, I'm your best friend, aren't I?
(MAUD *sits at the table.*)

LIZ

Yeah—of course you are. Come on, give.

MAUD

(*Eagerly, girl-to-girl*)
What do you say—let's take down our back hair, huh?

LIZ

Okay. Okay.

MAUD

Let's just be frank with each other, eh?

LIZ

Fine—shoot the works.

MAUD

Liz, dear Liz, get hep to yourself. The Duke just doesn't want you around. Among royalty—in court circles—you just wouldn't belong. You know—you'd look like a bum. And what's more—

LIZ

Maud! I'm your best friend, aren't I?

MAUD

You certainly are.

LIZ

And now that we've let our hair down I can be frank with you, can't I?

MAUD

Of course, you can say anything to me.

LIZ

All right. Keep your big mouth shut!
(*Blackout*)

SCENE 9

The afterdeck of the ship.
The upper deck is flooded with moonlight. The DUKE *is alone,*
leaning against the rail, presumably looking out over the water.
LIZ *enters, she looks up and sees him.*

LIZ

Hi, Hymie?

DUKE

Leez—how nice you are here!

LIZ

(*Looking out over the ocean*)
It's beautiful, isn't it?
(*The* DUKE *comes down the stairs, right.*)

DUKE

Perfect! The smooth sea—the path of the moonlight—the
white, straight avenue of foam from the propeller—

LIZ

(*Impressed*)
Yeah—romantic as hell! I'll go get Beth.

107

DUKE

No, no! Let her dance with her friends. As a matter of fact, I had been standing up there thinking of you.

LIZ

I'm not quite sure whether that's good or bad. What were you thinking? (*Then quickly*) Never mind—don't tell me.

DUKE

Why not, my dear friend?

LIZ

Skip it.

DUKE

You don't like me to call you "my dear friend?"

LIZ

That's all right. Just don't call me your best friend. I've found out that's not very friendly.

DUKE

I shall call you my *belle-mère*.

LIZ

Wait a minute! What kind of a mare?

DUKE

My *belle-mère*.

LIZ

(*Suspicious*)

You mean like a bell-cow?

DUKE

No, no. *Belle-mère* is French for mother-in-law. It means beautiful mother. A Frenchman calls his mother-in-law his beautiful mother.

LIZ

Very sneaky, those Frenchmen—very sneaky. In America it's practically illegal to like your mother-in-law. You're not supposed to want her around.

DUKE

How absurd!

LIZ

Hymie, I'm going to level with you. I don't want anything to be a roadblock to your marrying Beth.

DUKE

When I left my cabin after dinner, the Baron and the young man were hard at it, working—writing—fighting—

LIZ

Fighting? (*This gives her pause*) Hymie . . . my lawyer kinda hinted to me there might be an obstacle. I just want you to know—that if'n it's me—I can fix that.

DUKE

(*Puzzled*)
Leez, is there something? What is it?

LIZ

I'm just trying to tell you—I don't need to be around at all
except when you and Beth are in America. When you two are
abroad—you know, when you're around with royalty—I'd keep
away from you.

DUKE

Leez!

LIZ

And when it comes to the wedding—I could even arrange to
miss that. I wouldn't have to be there.

DUKE

What would you do? Have your clothes stolen? Leez, one of
the happiest things about all this is that you will be near.
(LIZ *turns to him, beaming. He kisses her and takes her
into his arms. Over the embrace we hear* LIZ's *thoughts,
again on tape.*)

LIZ'S VOICE

Good-bye, Mr. Livingstone!
(*They come out of the embrace.*)

LIZ

(*Glowing*)

Hymie—do something for me will you? Will you have somebody find Mr. Stewart and bring him here?

DUKE

Mr. Stewart? You want Stewart here?

HAPPY HUNTING

Yes, do you mind? Right away. Quick!
(*He gives her a puzzled look and exits*.)

(LIZ *sings, "This Is What I Call Love"*)
Look at me, I've got that proverbial glow
I'm not the dame that I was a minute ago
For the first time in my life
I'm throwing caution to the winds
For the first time in my life
My life begins.

I always knew it would arrive
This feeling of being the only two people alive
You and me
Now you're talkin'!
This is what I call love!

I almost feel like I could fly
I never knew that there were so many stars in the sky
And that moon
That's more like it!
This is what I call love!

When it's right
You know it's right
And everything else is amateur night

And when we kiss, then even more
I know I was just going through the motions before
Now at last

For the first time, darling
This is what I call love!

Not just a reasonable facsimile thereof
No, sir
This is what I call love.
> (HARRY *rushes on and goes to* LIZ.)

HARRY

Mrs. Livingstone, what's this about a statement?

LIZ

What statement?

HARRY

I hear there's going to be an announcement about the Duke and your daughter.

LIZ

Oh, no—not now—not now.
> (*The* DUKE *enters during her last speech.* HARRY *goes to him.*)

HARRY

Your Highness, what's this statement you're about to issue?

DUKE

Statement?

HARRY

That Baron of yours says he's about to give out a statement.
> (LIZ *starts to cross to the* DUKE. *She is cut off by the other reporters, rushing on.*)

JACK

(*To* HARRY)

Hi, pal, trying to beat us to something?

HARRY

Well, you can't blame a guy for trying.

(ARTURO *enters.*)

ARTURO

Your Highness, have I your permission to issue a statement?
(LIZ *moves away from the crowd*) Everything has been arranged as you wanted it.

DUKE

Very well, go ahead. (BETH *enters. The* DUKE *sees her*) Beth,
they're about to make the announcement.

(*He goes to* BETH's *side.*)

ARTURO

I have the distinguished honor to announce that a marriage
has been arranged between Miss Beth Livingstone of Philadelphia and His Royal Highness Prince of Hapsburg, Duke of
Granada, Count of Aragón—

(*The newspaper contingent goes into a series of excited
ad libs: "Where's the wireless room?" "What a story!"
"Come on, there's a ship-to-shore telephone." "It's one
deck below." "No, it's on the deck above." "This tops the
Kelly story!" "Baby, let's go!" "Where's my camera?"
"Why didn't they tip us off?" "Here we go again!" The
newspaper reporters and photographers rush off.*)

(LIZ *is standing alone. The passengers are surrounding
BETH and the DUKE, congratulating them. They are also*

singing excitedly to themselves and to BETH *and the*
DUKE *the number extolling the marriage of an American
girl to a Prince Charming.*)

(ENSEMBLE)

O, this fairy tale romance
O, the pomp and circumstance
(*Against this* LIZ *sings with quiet irony.*)

(LIZ)

And when we kiss, then even more
I know I was just going through the motions before.
(*The* DUKE *sees her, kisses* BETH'S *hand, and crosses to*
LIZ. *She stops her song.*)

DUKE

Well, Leez, it's official. Am I not to have a kiss, *belle-mère?*

LIZ

Please! Let's not add incest to injury!
(*She turns away from him.*)

Curtain

ACT TWO

ACT TWO

Scene 1

The garden of LIZ LIVINGSTONE's *home in Philadelphia. It is night, and a gay party in honor of the* DUKE *is in progress.* LIZ *has broken the social barrier. Main Liners, eager to meet His Highness, mingle with "commoners." Stage center, there is a rather small dance platform, and couples are dancing the tango to subdued music.* BETH *enters, looking about as though searching for someone. She encounters* ARTURO, *who has entered from the opposite side.*

BETH

Well, Baron, the Duke is late, so you'll have to dance with me.

(ARTURO *glances at the platform, which is beginning to fill up.*)

ARTURO

But I do not know this American dance.

BETH

This is a tango.

(*By this time the dance platform is so crowded that the couples are swaying but unable to move about.*)

ARTURO

A tango? For a tango in Spain, this wouldn't be room enough for one couple.

(They are now on the platform, poised for dance. BETH *starts singing, "A New-Fangled Tango.")*
We've got a new-fangled tango
And there's nothin' to it
You just sorta stand there
And just sorta do it

(ALL)
You cling close together
There's no wasted motion
A new-fangled tango
An old-fashioned notion

The floor may be crowded
But that doesn't matter
It's not necessary
To move, don't move, why move?
The floor may be crowded
But that's all the better
It's just like romancin'
While dancin'
(At this point, LIZ, *dancing with a* YOUNG MAN, *appears in the dance crowd.)*

LIZ
(Speaking)
Who's dancin'?
(Then she takes over the song)
Oh, you start off with one step
And cling to each other
And you know how one step
Can lead to another

118

Oh, there's nothin' wrong with
A waltz or fandango
But oh, what can come from
A new-fangled tango

All I'm sayin'
It's a good thing there's music playin'!

(ARTURO)
What a dance sensation
This could double the population!

(LIZ)
The floor may be crowded
But that doesn't matter
It's not necessary
To move, don't move, why move?
The floor may be crowded
But that's all the better
It's just like romancin'
While dancin'
Who's dancin'?

(*A* YOUNG MAN *in the dancing crowd bursts into song,
addressing his partner*)
You are like no other
You're for me—
    (*He examines his partner more closely*)
—Oh, my God, it's Mother!

(LIZ)
It's entrancin'
Why it's even more fun than dancin'!

119

(ALL)
Who's dancin'?

(LIZ)
There's no gettin' away from
The one big attraction
Oh there's not much movement
But there's lots of action

So give up the mambo
Forget the fandango
'Cause you'll fall in love to
A new-fangled tango

Your feet won't get tangled
Your nerves won't get jangled
And you won't get mangled—
A new-fangled tango!

(LIZ *turns. As she does so, she bumps the next couple.
They fall, striking another couple, who also fall, and so
on down the line until all but* LIZ *and her partner have
fallen. The dancers scramble to their feet.*

MRS. B. *and* MRS. D., *stalwarts of the Main Line, enter
separately and meet at a garden bench, right.*)

MRS. B.

How do you do, Emily?

MRS. D.

How do you do, Sophie?

MRS. B.

I'm surprised to see you here.

120

MRS. D.

I just had to meet the Duke. But you?

MRS. B.

Just curiosity.
> (*A third stalwart,* MRS. L. *joins them.*)

MRS. L.

That's the only possible reason.
> (MRS. STEWART *enters.*)

MRS. STEWART

> (*To* MRS. L.)

Why, Cornelia, you here?

MRS. L.

What about you, Letitia? I never thought you'd be a guest of Mrs. Livingstone.

MRS. STEWART

> (*Sitting on the bench*)

I don't think I should be criticized until I return the invitation.

MRS. D.

Letitia, do you really think this Duke has a chance of becoming King of Spain?

MRS. STEWART

Of course—it said so in the *Bulletin*. You know, we who really are Philadelphia should find some way to entertain the Duke.

MRS. D.

How can we do it and not invite the Livingstone woman?

MRS. B.

Mrs. Livingstone doesn't ride any more.

MRS. STEWART
(*Rising*)
That's good, Sophie.

MRS. L.

Yes, let's plan something with horses.
(LIZ *enters left.*)

LIZ

Girls, His Highness will be down in a minute. You've just got time to powder your noses.
(MISS W. *and* MISS S. *follow* LIZ *on.*)

MISS W.

Mrs. Livingstone, we've just seen him. He's divine.

MISS S.

He's the most.

LIZ
(*Wistfully*)
You don't have to tell me. I know.
(*The* DUKE *enters. He is wearing a white uniform, with gold trim.*)

LIZ

Everybody—I don't remember all your names—this is His Royal Highness, the Prince of Hapsburg, the Duke of Granada, and . . . I don't remember all his names, either.
(*There are excited murmurs of "Your Highness," and bows and curtsies.*)

YOUNG GIRL

Your Highness, may I ask you a question?

DUKE

Señorita, I love America.

MRS. B.

Your Highness—

DUKE

American women are the most beautiful in the world.

MRS. D.

Your Highness, I would like—

DUKE

It is not true, madame, American men do not spoil their women.

MAN

If you don't mind, Your Highness—

DUKE

Sir, your tall buildings—your skycratchers—most impressive.

LIZ

Didn't I tell you he was terrific? No wonder they want to run him for King of Spain.

MRS. STEWART

Your Highness, I'm Letitia Stewart.

DUKE

(*He goes to her*)

Yes, we met on shipboard.

123

MRS. STEWART

How nice of you to remember! Your Highness, we've been trying to plan a social occasion of some kind in your honor.

LIZ

(*Sotto voce, to the* DUKE)
What the hell does she think this is—a ball game?

MRS. STEWART

(*To the* DUKE)
Perhaps some opportunity for the Duke to show his horses. We know you're famous for your horsemanship, Your Highness.

DUKE

Nothing would give me greater pleasure.

LIZ

Say! I'll tell you what I'll do. I'll give a hunt for all of you.

MRS. B.

A hunt?

LIZ

Yeah, a fox hunt. What do you say to next Thursday? Seven o'clock in the morning. You're all invited.

MRS. STEWART

Mrs. Livingstone, you don't hunt foxes in the spring.

LIZ

Why not?

MRS. STEWART

They are mating.

LIZ

Not at seven o'clock in the morning.

MRS. STEWART

Really, Mrs. Livingstone!

LIZ

All right, if you're going to be sentimental about it— I've given enough money to the Philadelphia Zoo—they'll get me a fox that isn't married.

MRS. STEWART

But Mrs. Livingstone—you can't expect us to—

DUKE

(*With charming authority*)

I like Mrs. Livingstone's idea. It will please me. It isn't the fox that is the attraction in this particular hunt. Even abroad I have heard of the horsemanship of Philadelphia women—

MRS. D.

Oh, really!

MRS. B.

Well!

MRS. L.

In that case . . .

LIZ

Well, I guess that settles that!

DUKE

Nothing thrills me more than the sight of a woman on a horse.

LIZ

She has to be on a horse, huh?

DUKE

Well, not all the time . . . but, to me, if a woman doesn't ride . . . there is something missing.

LIZ

Well, I was just going to plan the hunt, I wasn't going to—

MRS. STEWART

(*Quickly*)

Mrs. Livingstone, we *must* have the hunt. You will ride with us, of course?

LIZ

(*Trapped*)

Oh, sure, what the hell!

MRS. B.

Your Highness, it has occurred to me that on the night of the hunt, the hunt ball should be in Spanish costume.

DUKE

Madame, I am honored.

MRS. STEWART

A ball? I wouldn't dream of going to a hunt ball in the spring.

LIZ

Mrs. Stewart, don't tell me *you're* mating!
(*The music starts.* BETH *enters. The* DUKE *goes to her,*

takes her to the dance floor where they dance. LIZ
watches them. A butler enters and whispers into LIZ'S
ear, then exits.)

LIZ
(*Distractedly*)
Huh? Oh, yeah. (*To the guests*) Come on, everybody. Sup-
per's served.
(*The guests start to exit, up left.* MRS. B. *turns to* LIZ *on
the way out, indicating* BETH *and the* DUKE, *who are still
dancing.)*

MRS. B.
Aren't they a handsome couple?
(LIZ *now follows the guests but keeps turning back to
look at* BETH *and the* DUKE. *Almost as soon as she exits
she reappears and calls.)*

LIZ
Hey, Hymie. Come and get it.
(*She exits again.)*

DUKE
Coming, Liz.
(*He and* BETH, *however, continue to dance.* SANDY *enters down left and sees them. He stops for a moment, as
if about to turn back, then squares his shoulders and
steps firmly onto the platform and taps the* DUKE *on the
shoulder. After a moment the* DUKE *surrenders* BETH *to*
SANDY. *The* DUKE *stands there, obviously with no inten-
tion of leaving. Finally,* BETH *breaks away from* SANDY,
takes the DUKE'S *extended arm and they exit, up left.*

SANDY *is left alone. He looks after them, then sings,*
"She's Just Another Girl")
She's just another girl
Like any other girl
I'd like to know just what's so special about her
I've known a million girls
A million zillion girls
Who were much smarter and a whole lot prettier

So what do I care what she does?
It's not my affair what she does
And that's just the way it should be
I mean, after all, she means nothing to me

But she is kinda nice
In fact, she's very nice
In fact, she very well might be for me paradise!
But what am I selling myself?
I've gotta keep telling myself
She's just another girl
Just another girl.

(*Blackout*)

SCENE 2

The LIVINGSTONE *stables. We see two stalls with their doors closed. Over one is a sign "Hero," over the other "Daisy." At rise,* TOM, MRS. LIVINGSTONE'S *groom, is sitting on a bench, cleaning harness. Near him is* TERENCE, MRS. STEWART'S *groom.*

TERENCE

You're positive now?—Old lady Stewart sent me over here to be sure they was going through with the hunt.

TOM

I didn't believe it myself until the fox was delivered today.

TERENCE

She's got a fox?

TOM

Well, it looks like a fox in the face.
(LIZ *enters. She is in a dinner gown.*)

LIZ

Good evening, Tom.

TOM
(Rising)

Good evening, ma'am.

TERENCE

Good evening, Mrs. Livingstone. Mrs. Stewart sent me over to make sure the hunt was still on.

LIZ

It's on, all right. And tell her nibs I'll have a ladder there to help her get on her horse.

TERENCE

Yes, ma'am. See you in the morning, Tom.
(*He exits.*)

LIZ

Tom, remember to have a ladder handy.

TOM

You don't mean that, ma'am—about the ladder?

LIZ

(*She looks around and lowers her voice*)
Yes, I do, Tom. I'm not sure I can get on a horse. I haven't been on one for eighteen years.

TOM

(*Surprised*)
You're planning to ride? A horse?

LIZ

Sh-h—(*Lowering her voice still further*) Daisy!

TOM

(*Almost shouting in surprise*)
Daisy!
(*We hear a kick against the wall of Daisy's stall and a long whinny.*)

LIZ

(*To* TOM)
I hope she didn't hear. I want to break it to her myself. (LIZ

strolls over to Daisy's stall) Tom, the Duke's down in the east wing with his horses. Ask him to meet me here before he leaves.

TOM

Yes, ma'am.
>   (*He exits.* LIZ *opens the top of the Dutch door of Daisy's stall and we see Daisy, a real live horse.*)

LIZ

Hi, Daisy! Are you feeling all right tonight? (*Daisy nods her head "yes"*) Is your cold better? (*Nods "yes"*) Feel fine, eh? (*Nods "yes"*) You used to be quite a hunter in your day, weren't you? (*Nods "yes"*) Do you think there's another hunt left in you? (*Nods "yes"*) That's great, Daisy—there's a hunt tomorrow morning. (*Daisy gives her a look*) I was thinking I might ride you. (*Daisy shakes her head a violent "no"*) Aw, Daisy—(*Shakes "no"*) Please, Daisy—(*Shakes "no"*) Daisy, you'd do that for me, wouldn't you? . . . Wouldn't you? (*Daisy shakes "no"*) I'm not doing any better with you than I did with Hymie. You haven't met him yet. Well, I'm crazy about him, but I found out a little too late. This love business is a funny thing, Daisy. It's a kind of a gamble. Like roulette, or betting on a horse race. You were a race horse once, weren't you? (*Daisy nods "yes"*) And men used to bet on you. (*Nods "yes"*) Sometimes they'd lose. (*Nods "yes"*) Well, it's the same thing, Daisy. Never bet on a man.
>   (LIZ *sings, "The Game of Love"*)
>   When the game of love begins
>   And the wheel of romance spins
>   Someone loses, someone wins
>   In the game of love

If you have your heart at stake
There's a chance your heart may break
But then that's the chance you take
In the game of love

Round and round and round she goes
Where she stops, nobody knows
I guess I'm just one of those
Who know the cost
I loved and lost

Once you've gambled, there's no cure
Some get rich and some get poor
One thing's certain, nothing's sure
In the game of love.

(*The* DUKE *enters, right.*)

DUKE

Leez—you wanted me?

LIZ

Yeah—isn't Beth with you?

DUKE

She is taking a walk in the garden. Are you ready to go back?

LIZ

Not yet—I wanted you to meet my horse. (*She sidles over to the* DUKE *and speaks confidentially*) Give her a build-up, will you? You know, butter her up. (*To Daisy*) Daisy—I want you to meet my friend Hymie.

(*The* DUKE *bows to the horse. Daisy nods.*)

132

DUKE

What a magnificent horse! Look at that head, that silky mane —Daisy, I must say you are a beautiful creature! (*Daisy modestly lowers her head*) It's a great pleasure to have met you.

LIZ

You know just what to give her—that old Spanish oil.

DUKE

Well, my *belle-mère's* mare is *très belle.*

LIZ

That's French, Daisy. *N'est-ce pas?*
(*Daisy nods.*)

DUKE

Which reminds me, when are you going to become my *belle-mère*—my mother-in-law?

LIZ

What's the big hurry?

DUKE

Well, at a Spanish wedding there is a custom. It is not the bride that the groom kisses.

LIZ

Oh! Who is it?

DUKE

His mother-in-law.

LIZ

No kidding—is that an old Spanish custom?

DUKE

It will be.

(*The* DUKE *exits.* LIZ *does the burnt-hand gesture.*)

LIZ

You see what I mean, Daisy? He's wonderful, isn't he? (*Daisy nods "yes"*) You wouldn't reconsider about the hunt, would you, Daisy? (*Daisy doesn't move*) Daisy—if not for me —would you for him? (*Daisy nods a vigorous "yes"*) Daisy— you're a daisy! (*She starts to close the door to Daisy's stall*) I want you to get a good night's sleep, Daisy—because I won't.

(*She closes the stall door. She starts out in the direction the* DUKE *has taken, singing as she goes*)

Round and round and round she goes
Where she stops, nobody knows
I guess I'm just one of those
Who know the cost
I loved and lost.

(*She stops and we hear her thoughts again on tape recording.*)

LIZ'S VOICE

Mr. Livingstone, you've got to admit it's tough. He's the only man I ever really loved and I've fixed it so he has to marry someone else. What does that make me?

(*We hear a violent kick in Daisy's stall and the entire door, both top and bottom, flies open, revealing a rear view of Daisy.* LIZ *turns and sees this.*)

LIZ

Who asked for your opinion?

(*Blackout*)

SCENE 3

A summerhouse on the LIVINGSTONE *estate.* BETH, *in evening dress, is moving about restlessly, obviously waiting for someone. Now and then she peers off into the darkness. Suddenly she starts to draw back and* SANDY *enters.*

BETH

Thank you for coming, Sandy.

SANDY
(Stiffly)

Well, you sent for me.

BETH

I just had to see you. (*She pauses for a moment to gather up her courage, and then blurts out what's on her mind*) Sandy, that contract you drew up between Mother and me and the Duke—is there any possibility of breaking it?

SANDY
(The calm lawyer)

None whatsoever.

BETH

Sandy, there *must* be.

SANDY

That contract is regarded by Lippincott, Lippincott, Drexel and Lippincott as the best contract ever drawn by Lippincott, Lippincott, Drexel and . . .

BETH

(*Cutting him off*)

Sandy, stop Lippincotting.

SANDY

Beth, as a result of that contract, they are making me a member of the firm. Mr. Lippincott said to me: "Stewart," he said . . . he knew my name! . . .

BETH

(*Cutting in*)

Sandy, would it help if I said I loved you?

SANDY

"Stewart," he said . . . I love you, too!—Oh!—

(*They embrace happily.* BETH *breaks the embrace.*)

BETH

Then you'll get me out of this?

SANDY

Well, there's something sacred about a contract.

BETH

Sandy!

SANDY

Don't forget, I'm a lawyer.

BETH

All right. I'll marry the Duke and you marry Mr. Lippincott.

SANDY

Of course, I'm a Philadelphia lawyer—and there's a way out of any contract. (*He thinks*) Let's see—could we have the Duke deported? We could get word to the Immigration Department that he's a wetback. No, we couldn't do that.

BETH

(*Firmly*)

All right, Sandy, *I'll* find a way myself.

SANDY

Wait a minute! The Duke could break the contract.

BETH

How can we get him to do that?

SANDY

You've got to go to him . . . tell him you don't love him . . . tell him you don't want to marry him. Under those circumstances, what else can he do but let you out?

BETH

(*Uncertainly*)

I don't know.

(*The* DUKE *strolls on from left.*)

DUKE

(*To* BETH)

Oh, there you are! I was looking for you. (*To* SANDY) Good

137

evening. (*To* BETH) I was just going back to the house. Are you coming along?

BETH

Not just yet, Hymie.

DUKE

Very well.
    (*He starts off.*)

SANDY

Just a moment, Your Hymieness—Your Highness—
    (*The* DUKE *stops and turns back.* SANDY *looks at* BETH *as if to say "Go ahead!"*)

BETH

Hymie—we have something very important to speak to you about—(*She turns to* SANDY)—haven't you?

SANDY

Yes—she has.

DUKE

So?

BETH

Well, Hymie—this isn't—easy to say— I—you see, I like you very much—really I do, but—

DUKE

Beth, you are trying to tell me that you don't love me.

SANDY

Yes.

138

BETH

(More weakly)

Yes.

DUKE

But I know that, my dear. Don't worry. (SANDY *and* BETH *smile at each other*) We will have a good marriage, you and I. (*The smiles fade*) We have one thing in common—our devotion to your wonderful mother. We must make her happy . . . not so?

BETH

But don't you believe in love?

DUKE

Do you know what makes so many unhappy marriages? Love!

SANDY

I must take exception, Your Honor—Your Highness. A marriage without love is no marriage.

DUKE

Nonsense. I can give you a hundred examples. The most successful marriage in my family was between my uncle Luis Alfonso and Princess Beatrice Maria. She was not speaking to him at the time of their wedding and she has never spoken to him since. They have been married fourteen years and have twelve children.

BETH

Fourteen years—and have twelve children.

SANDY

And she has never spoken to him? Never said a word to him?

DUKE

Well, occasionally, she must have given him a nod.
(*The* DUKE *gives them a salute of* au revoir *and exits.*)

SANDY

Beth—someone has to tell your mother that you don't love the Duke—that you love me.

BETH

Yes—but I couldn't be the one to tell Mother.

SANDY

Let's see—who could we get to tell your mother?

BETH

I don't know. Oh, Sandy!
(*He takes her in his arms. They kiss.* MAUD *enters, sees them, stops short.*)

MAUD

Oh! Oh, it's you!
(*The situation dawns on her. That "best friend" look takes possession of her face. She gathers up her skirts and goes off clippety-clop.*)

(*Blackout*)

SCENE 4

Outside the Hunt Club.
It is early morning, a few minutes before the start of the
hunt. We hear the neighing of horses and the barking of hounds,
offstage. The stage itself is crowded with men and women in
gay hunt clothes. They are standing about in groups, chatting,
many of them drinking stirrup cups. One of the groups, right,
includes MRS. STEWART *and the* MESDAMES L., B., *and* D. TERENCE,
MRS. STEWART'S *groom, enters and goes to* MRS. STEWART.

TERENCE

Your mount is here, ma'am.

MRS. STEWART

Thank you, Terence.
> (TERENCE *retires upstage and joins other grooms.* MRS.
> L. *speaks to* MRS. STEWART.)

MRS. L.

I think our idea worked out very nicely. Mrs. Livingstone
isn't here.

MRS. STEWART

Yes, we'll have the Duke to ourselves.

MRS. D.

It's clouding up. I wish we could start.

MRS. STEWART

We have to wait for His Highness.

(TWO MEN *who have had a good start on their stirrup cups approach.*)

FIRST MAN

(*Inspecting the sky*)

Looks like rain.

SECOND MAN

(*Inspecting his drink*)

Yes, but it tastes all right. (*He holds up his cup in a toast*) To the Hunt.

(*Some of the others pick up the line:* "*To the Hunt.*" *The music starts and the* MEN *begin the song* "*Happy Hunting.*")

(FIRST MAN)

Happy hunting

(SECOND MAN)

Happy hunting

(ALL)

Happy hunting
Tallyho, tallyho

(*At this point,* LIZ, *in hunting costume, enters and takes over the song*)

Tallyho

Everyone's on the hunt

For whatever they want
And whatever you want
Happy hunting
What a day for a hunt
Keep that eagle eye peeled
And look over the field
Happy hunting

That's what life is
Looking for the things
You haven't found
Don't just stand there
Look around, look around
Till you see what you like
And you like what you see
Be like me and you'll be
Happy hunting

    (ALL)
Everyone's on the hunt
For whatever they want
And whatever you want

    (LIZ)
Happy hunting

    (ALL)
What a day for a hunt
Keep that eagle eye peeled
And look over the field

(LIZ)

Happy hunting
That's what life is
Looking for the things
You haven't found
Don't just stand there
Look around

(ALL)

Look around
Till you see what you like
And you like what you see

(LIZ)

Be like me and you'll be
 (*Three grooms appear, one carrying* LIZ's *saddle.*)

(ALL)

Oh-o-o-o
Happy hunting!
 (LIZ *exits left with the three grooms. The crowd rushes over and looks offstage, watching her mount. Their actions indicate she is about "aboard" when suddenly they let out a dismayed "Oh!" There is sympathy for Daisy. Again their eyes are riveted offstage and again there is a dismayed "Oh!" This time one of the grooms dashes across stage left to right, the crowd watching him. He returns in a moment carrying a ladder. The crowd laughs and goes into a dance. Toward the end of the dance the grooms carry* LIZ *on, and they join in a soft shoe dance. The song starts again; the* DUKE *entering and joining* LIZ.)

HAPPY HUNTING

(ALL)
Everyone's on the hunt
For whatever they want
And whatever you want

(LIZ *and* DUKE)
Happy hunting

(ALL)
What a day for a hunt
Keep that eagle eye peeled
And look over the field

(LIZ *and* DUKE)
Happy hunting

(LIZ)
That's what life is
Looking for the things
You haven't found

(DUKE)
Don't just stand there
Look around

(LIZ)
Look around

(ALL)
Look around
Till you see what you like
And you like what you see

Be like me and you'll be
Happy hunting
Tallyho!

> (*Led by* LIZ *and the* DUKE, *the crowd exits, singing.
> The three grooms remain. They dance—suddenly there
> is a flash of lightning, a clap of thunder, and rain. Their
> riding crops turn into umbrellas and they exit.*)

(*Blackout*)

Scene 5

As the rain descends, a transformation takes place before the audience. A fence upstage disappears and a large rock appears. Men and women pass across the stage, participants in the hunt who have given up, running for cover with blankets and saddles over their heads: a man carrying a woman, a man limping. Then, against the backdrop, we see moving shadows of figures on horseback, first riding down a sharp hill, then taking a jump.

Suddenly we hear galloping hoofs. We hear LIZ's *voice offstage.*

LIZ

(Offstage)

Help! Oh, Mr. Livingstone, help!

(*The hoof beats stop suddenly. There is a scream and then* LIZ, *thrown from her horse, hurtles through the air and lands behind the rock. In a moment she is on her feet again, limping and rubbing herself. Her jacket is torn and her hat awry.*)

LIZ

That's one horse I'll never speak to again.

(*The* DUKE *rushes on from left.*)

DUKE

Leez—are you all right?

LIZ

Oh, Hymie, what will you think of me now?

DUKE

It wasn't your fault. That last jump—Daisy refused.
(FOUR MEN *in hunting clothes rush on.*)

FIRST MAN

Mrs. Livingstone, are you hurt?

SECOND MAN

That was a nasty spill.

LIZ

(*With doubtful bravado*)
Oh, it was nothing. A fall from a horse—that just adds to the fun.

DUKE

What a wonderful woman! I'll go catch Daisy and we'll go on. (*At this* LIZ *winces*) Tallyho!
(*He hurries off. The* FOUR MEN *pick up the song.*)

(MEN)

Tallyho!
Tallyho!

(LIZ)

Tallyhoooo!
(*Her hand goes to the spot where it hurts.*)

148

(MEN)
Let's go follow the pack

(ALL)
Let's go pick up the track

(LIZ)
And if I don't get back

(ALL)
Happy hunting
Tallyho!
(*The* MEN *exit.*)

(LIZ)
Tallyho!
Tallyho!
(*A fox's head appears looking over the top of the rock. It glances from side to side.*)

(LIZ)
Happy hunt—
(*She sees the fox.*)

LIZ
(*Speaking, to the fox*)
They went that way!
(*She points off in the direction the* MEN *have taken. The fox scoots off in the opposite direction.*)

(*Blackout*)

SCENE 6

A sitting room outside of LIZ's *bedroom in her home. There is a dressing table right and a chaise longue near it.* MAUD *is pacing up and down. A* MAID *enters, carrying a negligee.*

MAID

This is all pressed. (*With her head she indicates the bedroom offstage*) How's the jolly huntsman?

MAUD

She'll live. She's still in her boots and breeches.

MAID

Does she want me to help her out of them?
    (*She puts the negligee on a bench at the dressing table.*)

MAUD

No. She wants to wait till the skin grows back.

MAID

The groom was telling me about a wonderful liniment. Shall I go to the stables and fetch a bottle?

MAUD

Sure, go ahead.
    (*She starts as* LIZ *enters still in riding clothes.*)

MAID

Mrs. Livingstone, I'm going to the stables to get a bottle of liniment.

LIZ

Fine. And bring two glasses.
(*The* MAID *goes.* LIZ *paces up and down.*)

MAUD

Liz, why don't you sit down?

LIZ

You know damn well why I don't sit down. What about
you? Why don't you sit down?

MAUD

I've got something to tell you and I haven't got much time.
(*Looks at her watch*) I've got to get home and try on my Goya
costume.

LIZ

Your what?

MAUD

My Goya costume. It's what we agreed. We're each of us
coming to the ball tonight dressed as a Goya—you know, the
Spanish painter.

LIZ

I never heard of him.

MAUD

Liz, you kill me. You've got a fifty-thousand-dollar Goya
right downstairs in your living room.
(LIZ *looks alarmed.*)

LIZ

I can't go looking like that. We'd get raided.

MAUD

Not that one—the one over the mantelpiece.

LIZ

I'll go look.
(*She starts,* MAUD *stops her.*)

MAUD

Not now. I've got something to say to you—it's about Beth. Now, Liz, I hate to tell you this— Well, late last night on my way home from here, I passed the summerhouse and there were two people in there. It was Sandy and Beth, and they were kissing each other madly.

LIZ

Well, they're old friends.

MAUD

I wish I had a friend like that. Liz, Beth doesn't love the Duke.

LIZ

How could she help loving him? How could any woman help loving him?
(*There is a knock on the door.* BETH *opens it and enters.*)

BETH

Mother? (*She sees* MAUD) Hello, Mrs. Foley.

MAUD
(*Overpolite*)

Hello, dear, come in, come in.

BETH
(*Hopefully*)

I don't want to interrupt if you're telling Mother anything important.

LIZ

No, dear, nothing important. Is there anything you want to tell me?

BETH

Well, yes, Mother. I've just had a wonderful letter from Grace.

LIZ

Grace Kelly?

BETH

Yes, Mother. They never even knew we were in Monaco. That's why we weren't invited to the wedding. They're so sorry they missed us. They want us to come over and visit them as soon as possible. (BETH *hands the letter to a stunned* LIZ) And, Mother, they loved your wedding present. They're keeping it in France, for now, because there isn't room enough for it in Monaco.

MAUD

My God! What did you give them?

LIZ

A prefabricated summer palace.

MAUD

Well, they can always exchange it.

LIZ

(*To* BETH)

Beth, you go and write Grace and tell her we'll be glad to drop in on her. (*She hands back the letter*) Grace always was a nice girl.

BETH

(*Looking steadily at* LIZ)

You see, Mother, we didn't have to get even with the Kellys.
(LIZ *can't face her and drops her eyes.* BETH *exits. We
hear* LIZ'*s thoughts on tape.*)

LIZ'S VOICE

Mr. Livingstone, I shouldn't have done this—I shouldn't have
done this—not to Beth.

(LIZ *goes to the telephone, picks it up and presses a
house button.*)

LIZ

(*Into the telephone*)

May I speak to His Highness? . . . Hymie? . . . Could
you drop over to my wing and see me for a minute? . . . Yeah,
right away.

(*She hangs up.*)

MAUD

What are you going to do?

LIZ

(*As if facing an unpleasant chore*)

What can I do? For Beth's sake, I'll sacrifice myself. I'll
marry Hymie.

MAUD

When you fell off that horse, did you land on your head?
You, marrying the Duke!

LIZ

I've got to do it, whether I want to or not . . . and I want to.

154

MAUD

But, Liz, how on earth are you going to—?

LIZ

I'll just allure the hell out of him.

MAUD

You can't do it in those clothes.

LIZ

(*Looking down at herself in boots and breeches*)
Oh . . . the boots! Help me off with the boots. (*She sits gingerly on the edge of the chaise and* MAUD *struggles with one boot*) Hey, take it easy. (*She squirms on the chaise*) Take it easy, I tell you.

MAUD

I can't budge it.

LIZ

Skip it.
　　(*There is a knock on the door.*)

MAUD

(*Quickly getting the negligee and helping* LIZ *into it*)
Here, get into this. You've got to look feminine if you can.
　　(*There is another knock.*)

LIZ

Just a minute.

MAUD

Drape yourself on that chaise.
　　(LIZ *stretches out on the chaise, not without discomfort.*

Her boots protrude from under the negligee. MAUD *tries to stretch it to cover them. It doesn't work. She goes to the dressing table and rips the "skirt" from it and throws it over* LIZ.)

LIZ

Hey! What are you doing?
(MAUD *has taken a large jar of powder from the dressing table.*)

MAUD

Here—use plenty of powder. (*She powders* LIZ *profusely*) That makes you look pale and seductive. (*She surveys* LIZ) Well, pale, anyway. Be soft and clinging.

LIZ

Who? Me? Why?

MAUD

Well, you want to get him, don't you? Be delicate and lady-like.

LIZ

But Maud, that's not like me.

MAUD

That's exactly what I mean. For God's sake, don't be like you. (*There is another soft rap on the door*) Come in, Your Highness. (*The* DUKE *enters.* MAUD *speaks in a somewhat hushed tone*) Be gentle with her.

DUKE

Has anything happened?

156

MAUD

I'll let her tell you. She has a rather painful tale.
(MAUD *exits*.)

DUKE

Leez, what is it?
(*From here on,* LIZ *gives her own interpretation of femininity.*)

LIZ

Is that you, Hymie?

DUKE

Yes, Leez. Is something wrong?

LIZ

I'm utterly, utterly exhausted.

DUKE

Well, it was a hard ride today. I'm a bit tired myself.

LIZ

(*Invitingly*)
Would you care to lie down?

DUKE

(*Taking a chair*)
I'll just sit here. Leez, you were magnificent today.

LIZ

I didn't disgrace myself?

DUKE

Oh, no! The way you took those jumps—the way you got on your horse—and stayed on—Leez, you are an extraordinary

157

woman—(*He slaps her leg, hitting the boot. He looks at his hand and taps at the leg, mystified*) A very extraordinary woman.

LIZ

What were you saying, Hymie?

DUKE

I was saying how much I admired you.

LIZ

How nice of you to say so, Hymie. You didn't find it a vulgar display?

DUKE

Leez, what's the matter with you?

LIZ

What do you mean, Hymie?

DUKE

I've never seen you like this. You're sicker than I thought you were. I'd better call a doctor.
(*He reaches for the telephone.* LIZ *stops him.*)

LIZ

No—Hymie. But how sweet of you to be—how shall I say —so concerned about me.

DUKE
(*Furious*)

Leez, stop that!

LIZ
(*A little startled*)

Stop what, Hymie?

DUKE

Stop trying to be feminine.

LIZ

(*More determinedly feminine*)
Hasn't a woman the right to be feminine?

DUKE

Not your kind of woman. Leez, there are two kinds of women
—feminine and female, and you're female.
(*The "feminine" vanishes.* LIZ *jumps up.*)

LIZ

Female! That's a hell of a thing to call a woman.
(*She strides about, the flimsy negligee not hiding her
breeches and boots.*)

DUKE

Leez, look at you.
(*He laughs.*)

LIZ

What's so funny?

DUKE

I can see right through you.
(*She takes off her negligee, throws it down.*)

LIZ

Nuts to Maud! Nuts to you! Nuts to everybody!

DUKE

There! . . .

159

LIZ

I'm going to be myself!

DUKE

That's the woman I love.
(LIZ *stops short and looks at him.*)

LIZ

Hymie—what did you say?

DUKE

I said you're the woman I love. When you are you, Leez—
you're the woman I love. This is not according to the contract
—but you're the one I want.

LIZ

Oh, Hymie, let me sit down. (*She starts to sit, then remembers*) No, I'd better not.

DUKE

Am I maybe the man you want?

LIZ

Hymie—the minute I laid eyes on you, I flipped!

DUKE

(*Vehemently*)
Why didn't you tell me?

LIZ

Well, it's like you said—there are different kinds of women.
(LIZ *sings, "I'm a Funny Dame"*)
I'm a funny dame
Maybe I don't say I love you

Maybe sometimes I
Don't exactly show I love you
Though I'm not much at saying things fancy
I'm yours just the same

I'm a funny dame
Even though my heart is singing
Guess I can't say why
I just can't be soft and clinging
Sure, I know it's wrong
But that's how I am
I'm a funny dame.

DUKE

Leez, this is all too complicated. I don't want to talk about
what kind of a dame you are or what kind of a . . . a . . . guy
I am.
(*The* DUKE *sings,* "*This Much I Know*")
I don't pretend to understand the stars above
And there is much in this great world that I know little of
But if I'm sure of nothing else, I'm sure I need your love
This much I know
This much I know

I often wonder just what life is all about
And there are many, many times when I am filled with doubt
But, oh, your love is one thing that I cannot live without
This much I know
This much I know

I can't explain
Where could I start?

I only know
What's in my heart

I can't say what the future holds from day to day
And there are many roads to travel on along the way
But I'll be with you by your side, and, darling, there I'll stay

This much I know
This much I know

> (*The* DUKE *takes* LIZ *in his arms and kisses her pas-*
> *sionately. In a moment she comes out of the embrace.*
> *She gives the "burnt-fingers" gesture and picks up the*
> *song*)

> (LIZ)

How did it start?
I can't explain
I only know
I can't complain

> (LIZ *and* DUKE)

I can't say what the future holds from day to day
And there are many roads to travel on along the way
But I'll be with you by your side, and, darling, there I'll stay

This much I know,
This much I know!

> (*The* DUKE *is now on the chaise,* LIZ *standing behind*
> *him. She leans down, her head resting on his. Again we*
> *hear her thoughts on the tape recording.*)

LIZ'S VOICE

Oh, Mr. Livingstone, I never thought this could happen to me. He's class like you were. But what can he see in me? What have I got that would make him want me? Could it be my money? (*Her head comes up*) Why, of course—that's what it is! It's my money! Why the dirty louse!

(*She pushes the* DUKE *off the chaise.*)

DUKE

Leez, what is this?

LIZ

You'd do anything for a buck, wouldn't you?—You'd even marry me!

DUKE

But I want to marry you. I love you.

LIZ

Don't give me that—You love my money.

DUKE

Of course I love your money. I love both of you.

LIZ

I'm not going to be married for my money.

DUKE

Leez, that's very simple. We settle it this way. You give me all your money. I'll marry you anyway even if you haven't got a cent.

LIZ

(*Hurt*)

Oh, Hymie get out of here, will you?

DUKE

(*Indignant*)

Oh, I see, it is all right for me to marry your daughter for her money.

LIZ

But she doesn't love you! I do!

DUKE

Very well, Mrs. Livingstone, if you feel that way. But you are fooling yourself. I am not the pretender. You're the pretender!

(*He turns and exits. She calls out after he has left.*)

LIZ

Hymie!

(*She looks at the door. The music of "She's Just Another Girl" comes up.* LIZ *sings*)

But what do I care what he does?
It's not my affair what he does.
And that's just the way it should be.
I mean, after all, he means nothing to me.

But he is kinda nice
In fact, he's very nice
In fact, he very well might be for me paradise!
But what am I selling myself?
I've got to keep telling myself
He's just another guy
Just another guy.

(*Blackout*)

Scene 7

A corridor in the Hunt Club.
On stage are six flunkies dressed in eighteenth-century
Spanish costumes. HARRY WATSON *enters and is stopped by*
the FIRST FLUNKY.

FIRST FLUNKY
I beg your pardon—are you expected?

HARRY
I'm Harry Watson of the Chicago *Tribune*.
(JACK ADAMS *enters in time to save him.*)

JACK
Hello, Harry. Are you here to cover Liz Livingstone's Hunt
Ball?

HARRY
Yes. Chicago has decided to recognize Philadelphia. Who's
here?

JACK
Just the most important people in Philadelphia.

HARRY
At Liz Livingstone's party? Don't give me that! (*To the* FIRST
FLUNKY) On the level—who's here?

FIRST FLUNKY

Who's who.

HARRY

Who's Who's here?

JACK

That's right.
　　(They sing, "Everyone Who's 'Who's Who.'")

(ALL)

Everyose who's "Who's Who,"
Everyone who's "Who's Who's" here.

(HARRY)

Who's he?

(JACK)

Who's who?
Oh, he's "Who's Who."

(HARRY)

Who?

(JACK)

He

(HARRY)

Oh

(ALL)

Everyone who's "Who's Who"
Everyone here's "Who's Who"

(ALL)

There's the Drexels, the Littles
The Du Ponts, the Biddles
Van Scivers
MacIvers
The Bakers and the Wanamakers
Peters, the Pipers, the Pickerings, the Peppers
The Wideners, the Biddles, the Mellons, the Biddles
The Hackers and the Pennypackers
With a Biddle in the middle

Everyone who's "Who's Who"
Everyone who's "Who ooo"

(HARRY)

Who's he?

(JACK)

Who's who?

(HARRY)

Who's he?

(JACK)

Oh, he's her he

(HARRY)
Whose?

(JACK)
Hers

(HARRY)
Oh
Everyone who's "Who's Who's" here
And everyone here's

(JACK)
I know

(ALL)
"Who's Who!"

(*Blackout*)

SCENE 8

The Hunt Ball.
As the curtains part it is as though we had gone back a
hundred years or so. Everyone is in the dress of the Goya period.
They are engaged in a somewhat stately dance. MRS. STEWART
enters, in period costume.

MRS. D.

Letitia, how becoming.

MRS. L.

You should have lived in the eighteenth century.

MAN

Personally, I think she did.
(MAUD *enters, greeting everyone.*)

MAUD

Good evening. Good evening. Good evening. (*She comes*
face to face with MRS. STEWART) Good evening. Oh, I forgot.
You don't know me. (*A man bows, and indicates an invitation*
to dance) Oh, I'd love to.
(*They dance.* HARRY *enters and goes to* MAUD.)

HARRY

Hello, Mrs. Foley. I'm Harry Watson, the Chicago *Tribune.*
Remember me?

MAUD

I should say I do. Your paper ran that terrible picture of me. (ARTURO *enters, evidently perturbed. In his hand he has a cablegram.*)

ARTURO

Mrs. Foley, have you seen His Highness? Has anybody seen His Highness?

MRS. D.

No, we're all waiting for him.

ARTURO

I have just had a cable. There have been important developments in Spain.

HARRY

Yeah, I know. My paper had a tip on it from our Spanish bureau and I want to ask you—

ARTURO

I can not discuss the affairs of His Highness. Is there a place around here called Maryland?

HARRY

Maryland? Is the Duke in Maryland?

ARTURO

He telephoned me from there this afternoon.

HARRY

That's where people go to get married.

MAUD

Wait a minute. Beth was in Maryland this afternoon.

HARRY

How do you know?

MAUD

She was coming to my house for cocktails. She called to break the date. She called from Maryland.

ARTURO

(*Agitated*)

I must call Maryland and have them page His Highness.
(ARTURO *hurries off.*)

MRS. E.

Do you suppose Beth and the Duke have eloped?

HARRY

If they have, this could be a hell of a story.

MAUD

Impossible!

HARRY

Where's the telephone?
(BETH *and* SANDY *enter.*)

MAUD

Beth! We were just talking about you. They said you eloped!

BETH

I did.

MAUD

But where's the groom? (BETH *points to* SANDY. MAUD *starts off, right*) Liz! Liz!

HARRY

This *is* a hell of a story!
(*He rushes off.*)

MRS. STEWART

Sanford, is this true?

SANDY

Yes, it's true, Mother. This is Beth—Remember?

MRS. STEWART

Young lady, do I understand that you preferred my son to
the Prince of Hapsburg.

BETH

Yes, Mrs. Stewart, I did.

MRS. STEWART

You have a surprisingly sound sense of values.

BETH

Well, if'n I have, it comes from Mother.
(LIZ *and* MAUD *enter.* LIZ *and* BETH *go into each
other's arms.*)

LIZ

Baby, this is wonderful.

MAUD

Does the Duke know about all this?

BETH

He arranged the whole thing. He drove us to Maryland.

172

LIZ

Where is he?

BETH

Isn't he here?

SANDY

He started back long before we did.

BETH

He thought we should drive back alone.

SANDY

Yes, he put me on kind of a spot.

LIZ

(*To* MRS. STEWART)

Well, Letitia, we're sort of related now. This makes me your son's *belle-mère*.

MRS. STEWART

Mais oui, c'est vrai. Je suis enchantée, ma chère amie.

LIZ

N'est-ce pas.
(*They touch cheeks.*)

MRS. STEWART

(*To* BETH)

Come, my dear, I want to present you to my friends. You know Mrs. Foley, of course.

MAUD

(*Beaming*)

Champagne for everybody! (*The crowd exits.* MAUD *turns back to* LIZ) Come on, Liz. We have to drink to them.

LIZ

No, I'm worried about Hymie. What could have happened to him? You go ahead.

(MAUD *starts out. The* DUKE *enters with* ARTURO. MAUD *sees him and does a deep curtsy.*)

MAUD

Your Highness!

DUKE

You've been practicing.

MAUD

(*Pleased*)

Uh-huh!

(*She needs both hands to get up. She exits. The* DUKE *hands the cablegram he has been carrying back to* ARTURO, *who bows.*)

DUKE

Oh, Arturo, have somebody get my car out of the river.

LIZ

(*Going toward him a few steps*)

Hymie, if we're still speaking—

DUKE

I'm not so sure. After all, I was told to get out of here.

LIZ

(*With a smile*)

But, you didn't.

DUKE

Only because somebody had to do something for Beth. Her mother is very charming but not very bright.

LIZ

Oh, Hymie, you're wonderful. You're really a prince.

DUKE

There may be a question about that. Leez, I've had some news—news from Spain. My party—my followers—have informed me that I must marry someone of royal blood—if I marry a commoner they will not support my claim to the throne.

LIZ

Oh—(*She pauses*) Gee, Hymie, it's a good thing we didn't get together—you and me. You would have blown your chance to be king.

DUKE

You know, Leez, I don't think I ever wanted to be king. Maybe that's why I have been so much in love with danger. Too much.

LIZ

Hymie, you don't really mean that!

DUKE

Leez, I'll prove to you I don't want to be king. I will marry a commoner.

175

LIZ

Well, if you're determined to marry a commoner, I don't want to boast, but—

(*He takes her hand and kisses it.*)

DUKE

You're a very uncommon commoner. Leez, I want to stay here in America with you.

LIZ

But you can't be a "Your Highness" around here.

DUKE

I'll just be Mr. Hapsburg. And you'll be Mrs. Hapsburg.

LIZ

Mrs. Hymie Hapsburg! That sounds like a good American name!

(LIZ *and the* DUKE *reprise* "*Mutual Admiration Society.*")
We belong to a mutual admiration society

(LIZ)
My Hymie and me

(LIZ *and* DUKE)
We belong to a mutual admiration society

(LIZ)
I say, "Oh, you're the sweetest one"

(DUKE)
I say, "No, you're the sweetest one"

(LIZ)
He'll always be my favorite man

(DUKE)
I'll always be her biggest fan

(LIZ *and* DUKE)
The only fighting that we'll do
Is just who loves who more than who
And that's the way we'll pass the time of day
My baby and me
Oh, we belong to a mutual admiration society

(DUKE)
My baby and me.
 (*They are in a near embrace and* LIZ *feels the* DUKE's *wet coat.*)

LIZ
(*Speaking*)

Hymie!

DUKE
(*Singing*)

My baby and me.

LIZ

Hymie, you're wet!

DUKE

Well, my car skidded into the river.
 (*Singing*)
My baby and me.

LIZ

Hymie, you're shivering. I'm going to take you right home and put you in bed.

DUKE

Yes, I am a little cold.

(*The music continues as they turn and start off.* LIZ *turns and looks the audience square in the eye. The music stops.*)

LIZ

You can't let a man freeze to death.

(*The music starts again—and they exit arm in arm.*)

Curtain